Contents

Graham King   v

Introduction   1

Concise Dictionary of Abbreviations and Acronyms   3

Detailed Listings

American States and Territories: 2-letter postcodes   11

Canadian Provinces and Territories: 2-letter postcodes   26

Chemical Elements   28

E numbers   45

European Car Registration letters   145

UK Postcodes: Cities and Areas   200

UN – the United Nations Family   202

Browse Articles

Acronyms   5

Longest abbreviation   8

AMIAE, et al   12

Airline acronyms   14

Apocryphal acronyms   15

Basic   19

BSc and all those other Bachelors   22

Cabal   24

Creep   31

They're all Damn MADD!   34

Doctors' abbreviations   38

Points of the Compass   41

We're all jolly good Fellows!   50

ABQuiz   56

Gay	58
An abbreviation too far?	63
Ibid, idem, inf and other footnotes	70
The International Community	73
Internet abbrajargon	77
Initials	79
Jeevesian abbrevations	81
Jokey acronyms	84
Kt-KB3, B-KN5, Chess abbreviations	88
Lewd acronyms	94
Man through the ages	96
Money abbreviations from the Treasury	103
Abbreviations from the secret world	108
An initial quiz	114
OAPs and senior citizens	118
Oz abbros	122
Protests, organisations, rallies and causes	125
Poms, Pommies and POMEs	128
PIX, NIX and Varietyese	131
Portmanteau words	133
Mind your Ps and Qs	137
Some curious Qs	139
A question of being POSH	141
The Three Rs	152
Spoof acronyms	154
An abbreviated quiz	160
That's show business!	165
Smersh	169
Snafu and beyond	174
What's going to happen to SOS?	181
Truncated words	196
UIAA et al	208
The versatile V	232
Zip	234
And, finally, the AAA	234

COLLINS
WORDPOWER

Abbreviations and Acronyms
Graham King

This edition produced for The Book People Ltd, Hall Wood Avenue, Haydock, St Helens WA11 9UL

HarperCollins*Publishers*
Westerhill Road, Bishopbriggs, Glasgow G64

www.**fire**and**water**.com

First published 2000

Reprint 10 9 8 7 6 5 4 3 2 1 0

Cartoons by Cinders McLeod. Cinders McLeod's web site is at
http://freespace.virgin.net/cinders.mcleod

HarperCollins Publishers would like to thank Bob Coole for reading the text of this book.

ISBN 0 00 765996 2

A catalogue record for this book is available from the British Library

Typeset by Davidson Pre-Press Graphics Ltd, Glasgow G3

Printed and bound by Bookmarque

Graham King (1930-1999)

Graham King was born in Adelaide on October 16, 1930.
He trained as a cartographer and draughtsman before joining Rupert
Murdoch's burgeoning media empire in the 1960s, where he became
one of Murdoch's leading marketing figures during the hard-fought
Australian newspaper circulation wars of that decade. Graham King
moved to London in 1969, where his marketing strategy transformed
the *Sun* newspaper into the United Kingdom's bestselling tabloid;
subsequently, after 1986, he successfully promoted the reconstruction
of *The Sunday Times* as a large multi-section newspaper.

A poet, watercolourist, landscape gardener and book collector,
Graham King also wrote a biography of Zola, *Garden of Zola* (1978) and
several thrillers such as *Killtest* (1978). Other works include the novel
The Pandora Valley (1973), a semi-autobiographical account of the
hardships endured by the Australian unemployed and their families
set in the 1930s.

In the early 1990s, inspired by the unreadability and
impracticality of many of the guides to English usage in bookshops,
Graham King developed the concept of a series of reference guides
called The One-Hour Wordpower series: accessible, friendly guides
designed to guide the reader through the maze of English usage.
He later expanded and revised the texts to create an innovative series
of English usage guides that would break new ground in their
accessibility and usefulness.
The new range of reference books became the Collins Wordpower
series (see page 234), the first four titles being published in March
2000, the second four in May 2000. Graham King died in May 1999,
shortly after completing the Collins Wordpower series.

Introduction

Perhaps without our realising it, abbreviations and their smart cousins, acronyms, have become essential elements in our language and lives.

Unthinkingly, we use dozens, perhaps hundreds of them every day: BBC, BO, DJ, DIY, PDQ, M&S . . . ft, ins, lbs, ozs, kilos. Many of them have been in use so long we forget the actual words, phrases or names they represent: RSVP, QED, APC, BUPA.

Others, of more recent invention, hide fearsome medical terms we prefer to put out of our minds anyway, like Aids, BSE, TSS and CJD.

Acronyms – where the initials of a phrase or saying form a meaningful or pronounceable word – can be even more hermetic. How many of us would score ten out of ten for reciting correctly the full meanings of Oxfam, radar, scuba, Saga, Qantas, laser and Wasp? Or even Nimby, Serps, Miras and Tessa, which entered the language only a few years ago? Names of people, too, are abbreviated; you are forgiven if you don't know that RLS is the famous 19th century writer Robert Louis Stevenson, but how about GBS, FDR, JFK and JCB? Or Rab and Ranji?

Then of course there are those hundreds of work-horse abbreviations that save us so much time: mph, Herts, hippo, ie, nb, IOU, pm and so on. No problem here, because from an early age we learn how to recognise and use them. But there are hundreds more, those on the fringes of our lives that we see or use only occasionally, that we're not too sure about. Explaining the meaning of these seemingly unintelligible cutdowns is the real purpose of *Collins Wordpower: Concise Dictionary of Abbreviations and Acronyms*, and several thousand of them are listed here, mainly those that might cross the paths of the average citizen.

There are an estimated half a million abbreviations presently at large around the globe, so it might seem that this collection is but a drop in the linguistic ocean. But is your life likely to be bent out of shape by not knowing that AAPP is the Association of Amusement Park Proprietors, or that the ADMM is the Association of Dandy Roll and Mould Makers, or that behind the ABRRM lurks the Association of British Reclaimed Rubber Manufacturers? Or, if you are of a bucolic disposition, that ehm means eggs per hen per month? We think not, but if you disagree we will happily point you towards either Dr John Paxton's *Penguin Dictionary of Abbreviations* or the exhaustive *Oxford Dictionary of Abbreviations*.

The fact is, many abbreviations break into our lives and then, in time, pass out again, surviving only in erudite compilations such as the above. Will people, in a decade or two, know or care that TGIF means Thank God it's Friday, or that DINK means double income, no kids, any more than we know or care today that phren means phrenology and OSw means Old Swedish? Meanwhile, though, it probably pays to know the difference between el al and El Al, and you would drop a rather large brick if, at a social gathering, you confused a D&B with a D&C.

One final point, or period. All the abbreviations in this dictionary are printed without periods. Although this is a widespread trend, and one which avoids typographical fussiness while only on the rarest of occasions causing any ambiguity, you should know that the practice is not without its critics.

A

A	absolute (temperature); ace (cards); adult; advanced; ammeter (electric circuits); ampere; anode; area; atomic; (as in **A-bomb**); Argentine austral (currency); blood type A; excellence in exam marking); American; annual; answer; April; August; Australia
a	about; accepted; acceleration; acre; acreage; actual; address; adjective; afternoon; age; alto; *annus* = year; anonymous; answer; *ante* = before; area; arrive; arrived; arriving
A0-A10 etc	paper sizes, from the largest (**A0** = 841x1189mm; **A1** = 594x841mm) to the smallest (**A10** = 26x37mm). The standard writing sheet is **A4** = 210x297mm
A1	First class ships in Lloyd's Register; non-motorway arterial roads (eg **A2** from London to Dover)
AA	Alcoholics Anonymous; advertising agency; age allowance; Air Attache; American Airlines; Anglers' Association; anti-aircraft; Associate in Accounting; Associate in Agriculture; Automobile Association
aa	absolute alcohol; after arrival; attendance allowance; author's alteration (proofreading)
AA1	superior credit rating (finance)
AAA	Amateur Athletic Association (in England and

3

	Wales); Allied Artists of America; American Automobile Association; Australian Assocation of Accoutants; Australian Automobile Association; highest credit rating (finance)
AAAA	American Association of Advertising Agencies (also **4As**); Amateur Athletic Association of America; Australian Association of Advertising Agencies
AAAS	American Academy of Arts and Sciences; American Assocation for the Advancement of Science
AAB	Aircraft Accident Board
AAC	Agicultural Advisory Council; Amateur Athletic Club
AAEC	Australian Atomic Energy Commission
AAF	Army Air Force (US); Allied Air Forces
AAMI	age-associated memory impairment
AANA	Australian Association of National Advertisers
A&A, a&a	additions and amendments
a&h	accident and health (insurance); **a&i** = accident and indemnity
A&N	Army and Navy (Stores; Club)
a&s	accident and sickness (insurance)
AAP	Australian Associated Press; Association of American Publishers
A&R, a&r	artists and repertoire (entertainment industry)
aar	against all risks; average annual rainfall; aircraft accident report
AAS	Association of Architects and Surveyors
AAT	achievement anxiety test; Anglo-Australian Telescope (NSW)
AATA	Anglo-American Tourist Association
AAU	Amateur Athletic Union (US); Association of American Universities
AB	Human blood type (along with A, B and O); able-bodied seaman

ABA	Amateur Boxing Association (GB); American Bankers' Association; American Bar Association; Antiquarian Booksellers' Association; Association of British Archaeologists
ABBA	Swedish pop group (Agnetha, Benny, Bjorn, Anni-frid); Amateur Basketball Association
abbr	abbreviation
ABC	the English alphabet; American Broadcasting Company; Audit Bureau of Circulations; Associated British Cinemas; Australian Broadcasting Commission
ABC1s, C2s etc	JICNARS (qv) social grading of the National Readership Survey of Britain. A = upper middle class; B = middle class; C1 = lower middle class; C2 = skilled working class; D = working class; E = State pensioners, widows, casual and lowest grade workers
ABDP	Association of British Directory Publishers
ABF	Actors' Benevolent Fund; Associated British Foods
ABLS	Association of British Library Schools
ABM	Associate in Business Management; antiballistic missile
Abo	Australian aborigine
A-bomb	Atomic bomb (originally deployed over Hiroshima, Japan, in 1945)
ABPI	Association of the British Pharmaceutical Industry
ABRACADABRA	ABbreviations and Related ACronyms Associated with Defense, Astronautics, Business and RAdio-electronics. Name of original listing of space terms (US, 1960s)
ABRS	Association of British Riding Schools

Acronyms

An abbreviation or an initial becomes an acronym when the letters are pronounceable and the resulting creation is accepted into the language. Typical examples include **RADAR, QANTAS, WASP** and **NIMBY**. Some acronyms are however derived from compressed words, such as **OXFAM** (Oxford Committee for Famine Relief). Others, like **scuba** (Self Contained Underwater Breathing Apparatus) assume a life of their own as words for which the meaning of the initial letters are forgotten. (qv articles under *Jokey Acronyms; Airline Acronyms; Man Through the Ages; Apocryphal Acronyms and Lewd Acronyms*)

ABS	*anti-blockier* system = anti-lock brakes
ABSA	Association of Business Sponsorship of the Arts
ABT	Association of Building Technicians
ABTA	Allied Brewery Traders' Association; Association of British Travel Agents
ABV	alcohol by volume
a/c	account, or account current (bookkeeping term)
AC	alternating current; *appellation controlee* (quality control of French wines); Arts Council
ACA	Agricultural Cooperative Association; Associate of the Institute of Chartered Accountants (England and Wales)
ACAS	Advisory, Conciliation and Arbitration Service
ACC	Army Catering Corps; Association of County Councils
ACCA	Associate of the Chartered Association of Certified Accountants; Association of Certified and Corporate Accountants
ACGB	Arts Council of Great Britain
ACGBI	Automobile Club of Great Britain and Ireland
ACK	Acknowledgement
ACORN	A Classification Of Residential Neighbourhoods. A sampling system which divides the country into 38 neighbourhood types, from agricultural villages through inter-war semis to private flats
ACSN	Association of Collegiate Schools of Nursing
ACT	Australian Capital Territory; Advisory Council on Technology
ACTC	Art Class Teacher's Certificate

ACTT	Association of Cinematograph, Television and Allied Technicians
ACTU	Australian Council of Trade Unions
ACU	Auto-Cycle Union
ACV	actual cash value; air cushion vehicle
ACW	aircraft(s)woman
ACWS	aircraft control and warning system
AD	*anno Domini*: In the year of our Lord, ie, any time after the beginning of the first century (qv BC)

Anno Domini
CHRIST'S BIRTHDAY (AD)

ADAS	Agricultural Development and Advisory Service
ADC	aide-de-camp; analogue-digital converter
ADD	attention deficit disorder
ADHD	attention deficit hyperactivity disorder
Adidas	From the name of the German founder, Adolf Dassler
ADRA	Animal Diseases Research Association
Adv	adverb; advent
Advt	advertisement

ADCOMSUBORDCOMPHIBSPAC

ADCOMSUBORDCOMPHIBSPAC

Supposedly the longest abbreviation known in English, dating from the 1960s, and short for 'Administrative Command, Amphibious Forces, Pacific Fleet Subordinate Command'. The *Guinness Book of Records* lists a Russian acronym with 54 Cyrillic characters, which itself seems to call for a further abbreviation!

AEA	Atomic Energy Authority (GB); Actors' Equity Association (US)
AEC	Atomic Energy Commission (US)
AEROFLOT	Soviet Air Lines
AEU	Amalgamated Engineering Union
AEWHA	All England Women's Hockey Association
AEWLA	All England Women's Lacrosse Association
af, a/f	as found. Refers to the condition (usually poor) of an item in an auction catalogue
AFA	Amateur Fencing Association; Amateur Football Association; automatic fire alarm
AFAM	Ancient Free and Accepted Masons

AFASIC	Association For All Speech Impaired Children. A play on the term *aphasia*, the total or partial loss of ability to communicate
AFBS	American and Foreign Bible Society
AFIA	Apparel and Fashion Industry Association
AFL	American Football League
AFL-CIO	American Federation of Labor - Congress of Industrial Organizations
AFP	Agence France Presse
AFRAeS	Associate Fellow of the Royal Aeronautical Society
AFTRA	American Federation of Television and Radio Arts
Aga	*Aktiebolaget Gas Accumulator*, Swedish oven manufacturers
AGA	Amateur Gymnastics Association
AGB	Audits of Great Britain
AGBI	Artists' General Benevolent Institution
Agfa	*Aktieengesellschaft fur Anilinfabrikation* (Limited company for dye manufacturing)
Agitprop	A former Soviet Communist Party bureau for the dissemination of propaganda and agitation. Also **agitpop**, the use of pop music for political purposes
AGM	annual general meeting; air-to-ground missile
AGS	American Geographical Society
AH	*anno Hegirae*. After 622 AD, the Muslim dating system
ah ha!	American Holistic Health Association's newsletter
AHQ	Army Headquarters
AI	Artificial insemination; artificial intelligence
AIA	Association of International Accountants
AIAA	Association of International Advertising Agencies
AICC	All India Congress Committee
AIDAS	Agricultural Industry Development Advisory Service
AID	artificial insemination by donor; acute infectious disease
AIDA	advertising basics: Attention, Interest, Desire, Action

AIDS	acquired immune deficiency syndrome; aircraft integrated data system
AIH	artificial insemination by husband
AILAS	automatic instrument landing approach system
AIME	American Institute of Mining, Metallurgical and Petroleum Engineers
AIR	All India Radio
AIS	androgen insensitivity syndrome
AITC	Association of Investment Trust Companies
AJA	Anglo-Jewish Association; Australian Journalists' Association
AJC	Australian Jockey Club
aka	also known as
AL	American Legion
ALA	American Library Association
ALCM	air-launched cruise missile
ALCS	Authors' Licensing and Collecting Society
A-level	advanced level of education
ALF	Animal Liberation Front; automatic letter facer
A-line	Women's fashion shape: dress flaring from neck or waist
Algol	Algorithmic computer programming language
ALL	acute lymphoblastic leukaemia
Ally Pally	Alexandra Palace, London
ALPA	Airline Pilots' Association
ALPO	Association of Land and Property Owners
ALS, als	autograph letter, signed
aM	On the River Main (for certain German cities and towns)
AM; am	amplitude modulation; *ante meridiem*, or before noon; Albert Medal; Member of the Order of Australia
AMA	American Medical Association; Australian Medical Association; American Motors Corporation; Association of Management Consultants

American States and Territories

The following are the two-letter abbreviations used by the US Postal Service:

AL	Alabama	MD	Maryland	RI	Rhode Island
AK	Alaska	MA	Massachusetts	SC	South Carolina
AZ	Arizona	MI	Michigan	SD	South Dakota
AR	Arkansas	MN	Minnesota	TN	Tennessee
CA	California	MS	Mississippi	TX	Texas
CO	Colorado	MO	Missouri	UT	Utah
CT	Connecticut	MT	Montana	VT	Vermont
DE	Delaware	NE	Nebraska	VA	Virginia
FL	Florida	NV	Nevada	WA	Washington
GA	Georgia	NH	New Hampshire	WV	West Virginia
HI	Hawaii	NJ	New Jersey	WI	Wisconsin
ID	Idaho	NM	New Mexico	WY	Wyoming
IL	Illinois	NY	New York	CZ	Canal Zone
IN	Indiana	NC	North Carolina	DC	District of
IA	Iowa	ND	North Dakota		Colombia
KS	Kansas	OH	Ohio	GU	Guam
KY	Kentucky	OK	Oklahoma	PR	Puerto Rico
LA	Louisiana	OR	Oregon	VI	Virgin Islands
ME	Maine	PA	Pennsylvania		

AMEX	American Express; American Stock Exchange
AMF	Australian Military Forces
AMIEE	Associate Member of the Institute of Electrical Engineers
AMIMechE	Associate Member of the Institution of Mechanical Engineers
AML	acute myeloid leukaemia
AMP	Australian Mutual Provident Society
AMSAM	anti-missile surface-to-air missile
AMSTRAD	Alan Michael Sugar Trading (Company)
ANA	Article Number Association (issues bar code numbers)

ANC	African National Congress
anon	anonymous (usually refers to an author, unknown)
ANZAAS	Australian and New Zealand Association for the Advancement of Science

AMIAE, et al

When you see an abbreviation like this beginning with A, it is very likely that the A stands for 'Associate' – in the above case, *Associate Member of the Institute of Automobile Engineers*, There are several hundred scientific, professional and trade institutes which issue diplomas of competence; so many, in fact, that it is impracticable to list all but the most important in this desktop dictionary.

Anzac	Australian and New Zealand Army Corps (WW1)
ANZUS	Australia, New Zealand and US defence pact
AOB; aob	any other business
AOC	*Appellation d'origine controlee*
AOH	Ancient Order of Hibernians
AONB	Area of Outstanding Natural Beauty
AOP	Association of Optical Practitioners
AOR	album-oriented rock; album-oriented radio
AP	Associated Press (US)
APC	acetylsalicylic acid, phenacetin and caffeine in combination as a popular headache remedy
APEX	advance purchase excursion (a railway or airline reduced fare); Association of Professional, Executive, Clerical and Computer Staff
aph	aphorism
APH	The late author, humorist and MP Sir Alan Herbert
APHI	Association of Public Health Inspectors
APLE	Association of Public Lighting Engineers
APR	annual percentage rate
APT	Advanced Passenger Train; automatic picture transmission
APTIS	All Purpose Ticket Issuing System

APU	Assessment Performance Unit (educational research unit)
ar; arr	arrives; arrived
AR	*anno regni* (in the year of the reign of)
Aramco	Arabian-American Oil Company
ARC	Aids-related complex
arch	archaism; archaic; architect; architecture
ARCS	Associate of the Royal College of Science
ARSR	air route surveillance radar
artic	articulated vehicle
AS	air speed
ASA	Advertising Standards Authority; Amateur Swimming Association; American Standards Association (photographic speed rating)
ASCII	American Standard Code for Information Interchange
asap	as soon as possible
ASEAN	Association of South-East Asian Nations (Indonesia, Malaysia, Thailand, Singapore, Philippines)
ASH	Action on Smoking and Health
ASIO	Australian Security Intelligence Organisation
ASLEF	Associated Society of Locomotive Engineers and Firemen
ASM	assistant sergeant-major; assistant sales manager; assistant scout master; assistant stage manager; air-to-surface missile
ASN	average sample number
ASO	American Symphony Orchestra
ASPCA	American Society for the Prevention of Cruelty to Animals
ASPEP	Association of Scientists and Professional Engineering Personnel
ASPF	Association of Superannuation and Pension Funds
ASR	airport surveillance radar
AST	Atlantic Standard Time
AT&T	American Telephone & Telegraph Company
ATC	air traffic control; Air Training Corps

ATD	Art Teacher's Diploma; actual time of departure
ATHE	Association of Teachers in Higher Education
ATM	automatic teller machine
ATO	assisted take-off

Airline Acronyms

Although Delta is the only airline listed in the dictionary with a spoof acronym (Don't Expect Luggage To Arrive) there are, apparently, many more, most of them the wicked inventions of frustrated passengers. American acronymaniac Don Hauptman reports these lethal one-liners:

TWA	Try Walking Across (also The Worst Airline)
ALITALIA	Always Late In Takeoff, Always Late In Arriving
EL AL	Embark Late, Arrive Late
BWIA	But Will It Arrive?
SABENA	Such A Bad Experience, Never Again!

BOAC, now British Airways, became the devastating acronym for Better On A Camel, and Delta earned a second stinging acrobarb: Doesn't Even Leave The Airport.

ATOL	Air Travel Organisers' Licence
ATS	Auxiliary Territorial Service, precursor of the present-day women's army, the **WRACs**
ATV	Associated Television
AUBTW	Amalgamated Union of Building Trade Workers
AUEW	Amalgamated Union of Engineering Workers
Auk	Field Marshal Sir Claude Auchinleck (WW2)
AUO	African Unity Organisation
AUT	Association of University Teachers
Auth Ver	Authorized Version of the Bible (also **AV, av**)
Aux, aux	auxiliary
AV	audio-visual
Av, Ave, ave	avenue
Av, Avg, avg	average
AVR	Army Volunteer Reserve

Avro	Former British aircraft maker founded by A V Roe
AVS	Anti-Vivisection Society

AVS   ANTI-VIVISECTION SOCIETY

AWA	Amalgamated Wireless (Australasia) Ltd
AWACS	airborne warning and control system
AWBA	American World's Boxing Association
AWGIE	Award presented by the Australian Writers' Guild
AWOL	absent without leave
AWRE	Atomic Weapons Research Establishment
AZT	azidothymidine (Zidorudine), a drug used to supress HIV, the cause of Aids (qv)

Apocryphal Acronyms

Many well-known names harbour acronymic myths. *Cabal, posh* and *pom* are examples (see listing under CABAL, POSH and POMS).

That TANZANIA is a blend of the former African countries Tanganyika and Zanzibar is true, but the notion that PAKISTAN is an acronym of the Indian provinces it united is pure whimsy. The Punjab, the Afghan border region, KashmIr, Sind and BaluchisTAN certainly do form a coincidental acronym, Pakistan, but it doesn't really wash; Kashmir was never included in the country that was founded in 1947. To Muslims, Pakistan means 'holy land'.

SCROD is a fish on many restaurant menus, especially in the US. Know-alls have long insisted that it is not a species of fish but an acronym of Special Catch Received On Dock; that is, the miscellaneous haul of the day, whatever it is. In fact *scrod* is a young Atlantic cod or haddock and its name derives from the practice of splitting it upon landing ready for cooking (from the Dutch *schrode*, to strip).

An intriguing myth surrounds the ENOLA GAY, the name of the aircraft that dropped the world's first atomic bomb on Hiroshima on 6 August, 1945. It is supposedly a reverse acronym of You Are Going ALONE. The truth is that the bomber was named after Mrs Enola Gay Tibbets, the mother of the pilot, Colonel Paul Tibbets.

Effeminate men are commonly described as *camp* ("He's as camp as a row of tents, dahling!") with the traditional acceptance that the term derives from KAMP, the police abbreviation for Known As Male Prostitute. There is no evidence for this assumption so it must remain an acronymic myth, as must the notion that COP is an acronym of Constable On Patrol.

The derogatory WOG and WOP have long been assumed to be acronyms of Westernised Oriental Gentleman (or more euphemistically, Workers On Government Service) and Without Official Papers. Etymologists regard these origins as extremely doubtful so they remain as apocryphal acronyms.

B

B	Thai baht (currency); Baumé (temperature); human blood type (of the ABO group); grade of softness in pencils (eg **2B**, **3B** etc); American bomber series (eg **B-52**); battle; bishop (chess); breathalyser; bold; bachelor; Baptist; billion; British; occupational group (of ACB1C2 etc); building; Venezuelan bolivar (currency)
b	ball, batsman, bowled, bye (cricket); base; bass; bath; bedroom; before; billion; book; born; bound (bookbinding); bowels; breadth; by; euphemism for bloody, bugger
B0, B5 etc	series of paper sizes (qv **A0-A10** etc)
B4216 etc	secondary roads (qv **A1, M1**)
BA	Bachelor of Arts; British Airways; British Academy; able-bodied seaman; Booksellers' Association; British Association for the Adancement of Science (also **BAAS**); bronchial asthma; Buenos Aires; bank acceptance; British Association screw thread
BAA	British Airports Authority; Bachelor of Applied Arts; Booking Agents' Association of Great Britain; British Archaelogical Association; British Astronomical Association
BAA&A	British Assocation of Accoutants and Auditors
BAAB	British Amateur Athletic Board

BA(Admin)	Bachelor of Arts in Administration (also **BAdmin**)
BAAF	British Agencies for Adoption and Fostering
BA(Art)	Bachelor of Arts in Art
BAAS	British Association for the Advancement of Science (also **BA**)
Bab	Babylonian
BABIE	British Association for the Betterment of Infertility and Education
BABS	Blind Approach Beacon System (airports)
Bac, bac	*baccalaureat* = study programme similar to British A-levels, a prerequisite for University entrance
BAC	British Aircraft Corporation; blood-alcohol concentration; British Association of Chemists
BACO	British Aluminium Company
BACS	Bankers' Automated Clearing Service
bact	bacteria; bacteriology
BADA	British Antique Dealers' Association
BAe	British Aerospace
BAEA	British Actors' Equity Association
BAEC	British Agricultural Export Council
BA(Econ)	Bachelor of Arts in Economics
BA(Ed)	Bachelor of Arts in Education
BAFO	British Army Forces Overseas
BAFTA	British Academy of Film and Television Arts
BAGA	British Amateur Gymnastics Association
BAgr	Bachelor of Agriculture; **BAgEc** = Bachelor of Agricultural Economics; **BAgrSc** = Bachelor of Agricultural Science)
Bah	Bahamas
BAHOH	British Association for the Hard of Hearing
BAI	Bachelor of Engineering
BAIE	British Association of Industrial Editors
Ball, Bal	Balliol College (Oxford); Ballarat (Victoria)
BALPA	British Airline Pilots' Association
b&b	bread and breakfast
BARC	British Automobile Racing Club
Bart's	St Bartholomew's Hospital, London

Basic

BASIC is the acronym for British, American, Scientific, International, Commercial language. Intended as a global language it was created in 1929 by C K Ogden and I A Richards with a vocabulary of just 850 common words. However, most people today recognise **BASIC** as a computer programming language and the acronym for Beginners' All-purpose Symbolic Instruction Code.

BAT	British-American Tobacco Company
Bat, bat	battalion; battery
BAWA	British Amateur Wrestling Association
BB	Brigitte Bardot; very soft black lead pencil; pseudonym of prolific English country book author and illustrator Denys Watkins-Pitchford (1905-1990).
BBBC	British Boxing Board of Control
BBC	British Broadcasting Corporation
BBFC	British Board of Film Censors
bbl	barrel; **bbls/d** = barrels per day (usually of oil production)
BBQ	barbecue
BC	Before Christ; British Council; British Colombia, Canada
bcc	blind carbon copy, i.e. one that the recipient of the original message is unaware of
BCCI	Bank of Credit and Commerce International
BCF	British Chess Federation
BCNZ	Broadcasting Corporation of New Zealand
BCom	Bachelor of Commerce
BD	Bachelor of Divinity
BDA	British Dental Association; British Dyslexia Association
BDD	body dismorphic disorder – a preoccupation with a perceived defect in appearance, causing distress and impairment in functioning.
BDS	Bachelor of Dental Surgery
BEA	British European Airways

BE	British Empire
BEd	Bachelor of Education
Beds	Bedfordshire
BEEB	British Broadcasting Corporation (also **BBC**)
BEF	British Expeditionary Force
Bee Gees	From Brothers Gibb, family pop group
BEM	British Empire Medal
Benelux	Customs union between Belgium, the Netherlands and Luxembourg
BEng	Bachelor of Engineering
Berks	Berkshire
BeV	unit of one billion electron volts
BFG	big friendly giant
BFPA	British Film Producers' Association
BFPO	British Forces Post Office
BHS	British Home Stores; British Horse Society
Bib	Bible; Biblical
bibl	bibliography; bibliographical
BIET	British Institute of Engineering Technology
Biggles	Code for 'Biggles Flies Undone'
BIM	British Institute of Management
BIOS	Basin Input / Output System
BISF	British Iron and Steel Federation
Bit, bit	binary digit (BInary digiT)
BL	Bachelor of Law
B/L, b/l	bill of lading
BLitt	Bachelor of Letters
BLL	Bachelor of Laws
BLT, blt	bacon, lettuce and tomato (sandwich); built
blvd	boulevard
BMJ	*British Medical Journal*
B-movie	Low-cost supporting movie (originally Hollywood productions)
BMT	British Mean Time; bone marrow transplant
BMTA	British Motor Trade Association

BMus	Bachelor of Music
BMW	*Bayerische Motoren Werke*, Bavaria: car manufacturer
BMX	bicycle motocross; a bicycle designed for rough or stunt riding
bn	billion
BNA	British Nursing Association
BNFL	British Nuclear Fuels Limited
BO, bo	body odour; box office
BOAC	British Overseas Airways Corporation
Bod	Bodleian Library, Oxford
BOLTOP	better on lips than on paper (usually placed below a 'paper kiss' – X – on the back of a lover's envelope)
BOOK	box of organised knowledge (Anthony Burgess's definition of a book)
BOP	*Boy's Own Paper* (boy's weekly, 1879-1967)
BOSS	Bureau of State Security (South Africa)
BOT	Board of Trade
bot	botany; botanical; bottle; bottom
BOTB	British Overseas Trade Board
BP	British Petroleum
B-P	Lord Baden-Powell, founder of the Scout movement
BPA	British Philatelic Association
BPC	British Pharmaceutical Codex; British Printing Corporation
bpm	beats per minute (heart rate)
BPS	British Pharmacological Society; bits per second
B&Q	DIY chain store established by a Mr Block and a Mr Quayle in Southampton in 1968
br	branch; bridge; brown
BR	British Rail
bra	brassiere
BRCS	British Red Cross Society
Brig	Brigadier; **Brig Gen** = Brigadier General
BRM	British Racing Motors

Bro, bro	Brother; brother
B-road	secondary road
BS	bullshit
BSC	British Safety Council; British Steel Corporation; British Sugar Corporation; British Standards Council
BSc	Bachelor of Science

BSc and all those other Bachelors

The original handful of university Bachelor degrees has in recent years proliferated to hundreds: **BLE** (Bachelor of Land Economy); **BNSc** (Bachelor of Nursing Science); **BO** (Bachelor of Oratory); **BPd** (Bachelor of Pedagogy) and so on. There are dozens of specialist arts degrees, too: **BA(Arts); BA(Econ); BA(Theol)**, etc; and scores of variations on science degrees: **BSc(H Ec); BSc(Med Lab Tech)** – of which only the most significant are listed in this desktop dictionary.

BSCP	British Standard Code of Practice
BSE	bovine spongiform encephalopathy ('mad cow' disease)
BSG	British Standard Gauge (railways)
BSI	British Standards Institution
B-side	The 'flip' or less important side of a vinyl record
BSkyB	British Sky Broadcasting (an amalgamation of **Sky TV** and **BSB**, British Satellite Broadcasting)
BSRA	British Sound Recording Association
BSSc	Bachelor of Social Science (sometimes **BSocSc**)
BST	British Summer Time
Bt, Bart	Baronet
BTC	British Transport Commission
btl	bottle
BTU	British Thermal Unit
BTW	by the way
Bucks	Buckinghamshire
BUPA	British United Provident Association

BURMA   be undressed, ready, my angel (on lover's envelope)

BURMA   BE UNDRESSED, READY, MY ANGEL

BV	*Besloten Vennootschap* (private company in Holland)
BVDs	Mens' one-piece underwear originally made by the US firm Bradley, Voorhees & Day
BVI	British Virgin Islands
b/w	black and white; monochrome
BWA	British West Africa
BWIA	British West Indies Airways
BWM, bwm	burst water main
BWV	*Bach Werke-Verzeichnis* (numbered catalogue of the works of J S Bach, first published in 1950)
BYO, byo	bring your own; **BYOB** = bring your own bottle/beer
Byz	Byzantine

C

Cabal

The story goes that the word *cabal* (a secret clique) derives from an acronym made up of the first letters of the names of five ministers of Charles II who signed an infamous treaty in 1672 – Clifford, Ashley Cooper, Buckingham, Arlington and Lauderdale. It's a good story but not true; that the initials form the word is coincidental. *Cabal* derives from the Hebrew *qabbala*, meaning 'secret doctrines'.

C	degree of heat in Celsius or centigrade; Carboniferous (geology); capacitance (physics); Cape; American series of cargo aircraft, (eg **C-10**); Catholic; Celtic; century; Roman numeral for 100; euphemism for cancer; cocaine; *calle* = street (Spanish); canon; canto; Captain; Cardinal; chief; Christian; circuit; club (cards); Conservative; copyright; coulomb; Commodore; Corps; council; Count; County; cold
c	carat; capacity; carbon; catcher (baseball); caught (cricket); cent; centavo; centime; centre; century; chapter; child; church; circuit; *circa* = about (eg c1850); city; cloudy; cold; colt; commended; contralto; copy; copyright; council; county; coupon; court; cousin; crowned; cubic; curate; curacy; currency; cycle

C1	supervisory or clerical occupational category (ABC1C2 etc)
C2	skilled or responsible manual worker occupational category
C3	low grade physical fitness category
C4	Channel Four Television
c/-	care of (also **c/o**)
CA	Consumers' Association; capital allowances; Caterers' Association; Central America; Certificate of Airworthiness; *chargé d'affaires*; Chartered Accountant; chronological age; civil aviation; Companies Act; *Corps d'Armée* = Army Corps; Chief Accountant; Court of Appeal; Croquet Association; Crown Agent; current assets
C/A	capital account; credit account; current account
Ca	Canada; Canadian; *compagnia* = company (Italy)
Ca	*circa* = about (qv **c**); close annealed
CAA	Civil Aviation Authority; Capital Allowances Act; Clean Air Act; Civil Aeronautics Administration (US); County Agricultural Advisor
CAB	Citizens' Advice Bureau; Canadian Association of Broadcasters
cab	taxi (from *cabriolet*); cabin; cabinet; cable
CAC	Central Advisory Committee; Consumer Advisory Council (US)
CAD	Crown Agents Department; computer-aided design
CAE	computer-aided education; computer-aided engineering; College of Advanced Education (Australian)
Caern	Caernarvonshire
CAF	Central African Federation; cost and freight (also **caf, cf, c&f**)
CAFE	corporate average fuel economy (US fuel consumption standard)
CAG	Concept Artists' Guild; Composers'-Authors' Guild
CAH	chronic active hepatitis

CAI	Club Alpino Italiano; Canadian Aeronautical institute
CAL	computer-assisted learning; Cornell Aeronautical Laboratory (US)
Cal	Calcutta; Caledonia
cal	calibre; calendar; calorie
CALPA	Canadian Air Line Pilots' Association
CALTEX	California Texas Petroleum Corporation
CAM	computer aided manufacturing
Camb	Cambrian, Cambridge
Cambs	Cambridgeshire
CAMRA	Campaign for Real Ale

Canadian Provinces and Territories Abbreviations

These are the two-letter abbreviations used by the Canadian Postal Service for its provinces and territories:

AB	Alberta	NT	Northwest Terr	PE	Prince Edward Is
BC	British Colombia	NS	Nova Scotia	PQ	Quebec
LB	Labrador	ON	Ontario	SK	Saskatchewan
MB	Manitoba	NB	New Brunswick	UT	Yukon Territory
NF	Newfoundland				

canc	cancelled; cancellation
C&A	Chain stores named after Dutch brothers Clemens and Auguste Breeninkmeyer
C&M	care and maintenance
Cant	Canterbury
Cantab	Cambridge (from the Latin *Cantabrigiensis*)
CAP	Common Agricultural Policy (EU)
Cap. cap	capital city; capacity; capital letter; captain (also **Capt**)
Card	Cardinal
CARE	Cooperative for American Relief to Europe (after WW2)
carr	carriage
CARICOM	Caribbean Community and Common Market
CARIFTA	Caribbean Free Trading Area

cat	catalogue
Cath	Catholic; cathedral
CATNYP	Catalogue of the New York Public Library
CATS	Student's credit accumulation transfer scheme
CATscan	computerised axial tomography (body scan)
C&W	country and western (music)
CATV	cable/community antenna
CAVU	Ceiling and Visibility Unlimited (aviation)
CB	citizens' band (radio frequency); Companion of the Order of the Bath
CBC	Canadian Broadcasting Corporation
CBE	Commander of the Order of the British Empire
CBI	Confederation of British Industries
cbk	cheque-book
CBS	Columbia Broadcasting System
CBSO	City of Birmingham Symphony Orchestra
CC	Cricket/Croquet/Cruising/Cycling Club; City Council; County Council
cc	carbon copy; cubic centimetre
c&c	curtains and carpets
CCC	Central Criminal Court, London (Old Bailey)
CCCP	Union of Soviet Socialist Republics
CCITT	*Comite Consultatif International Telegraphique et Telephonique* (UN telecommunications committee in Geneva)
CCP	Chinese Communist Party
CCTV	closed circuit television
CD	compact disc; Corps Diplomatique
cd fwd	carried forward
CD-R	compact disc that can be recorded on once
CD-ROM	compact disc – read-only memory
CD-RW	compact disc that be recorded on over and over
CDT	Central Daylight Time (North America)
CDV	compact video disc
CE	Church of England; chief engineer; civil engineer; Common Entrance (exam)

The Chemical Elements

Ac	actinium	Au	gold	Pm	promethium
Al	aluminium	Hf	hafnium	Pa	protoactinium
Am	americium	He	helium	Ra	radium
Sb	antimony	Ho	holmium	Rn	radon
Ar	argon	H	hydrogen	Re	rhenium
As	arsenic	In	indium	Rh	rhodium
At	astatine	I	iodine	Rb	rubidium
Ba	Barium	Ir	iridium	Ru	ruthenium
Bk	berkelium	Fe	iron	Sm	samarium
Be	beryllium	Kr	krypton	Sc	scandium
Bi	bismuth	La	lanthanum	Se	selenium
B	boron	Lr	lawrencium	Si	silicon
Br	bromine	Pb	lead	Ag	silver
Cd	cadmium	Li	lithium	Na	sodium
Cs	caesium	Lu	lutetium	Sr	strontium
Ca	calcium	Mg	magnesium	S	sulphur
Cf	californium	Mn	manganese	Ta	tantalum
C	carbon	Md	mendelevium	Tc	technetium
Ce	cerium	Hg	mercury	Te	tellurium
Cl	chlorine	Mo	molybdenum	Tb	terbium
Cr	chromium	Nd	neodymium	Tl	thallium
Co	cobalt	Ne	neon	Th	thorium
Cb	columbium	Np	neptunium	Tm	thulium
Cu	copper	Ni	nickel	Sn	tin
Cm	curium	Nb	niobium	Ti	titanium
Dy	dysprosium	N	nitrogen	W	tungtsen
Es	einsteinium	Os	osmium	U	uranium
Er	erbium	O	oxygen	V	vanadium
Eu	europium	Pd	palladium	Xe	xenon
Fm	fermium	P	phosphorus	Yb	ytterbium
F	fluorine	Pt	platinum	Y	yttrium
Fr	francium	Pu	plutonium	Zn	zinc
Gd	gadolinium	Po	polonium	Zr	zirconium
Ga	gallium	K	potassium		
Ge	germanium	Pr	praseodymium		

CET	Central European Time
cf	compare; calf (bookbinding); centre foward (football); centre fielder (baseball)
c/f	carried forward
CFC	chlorofluorocarbon gases
cfi	cost, freight and insurance
CFS	chronic fatigue syndrome (see ME)
cg	centigram; centre of gravity
CGA	Country Gentlemen's Association
cgt	capital gains tax
ch	chain; chapter; chairman or chair
Ches	Cheshire
chq	cheque
Chi	Chicago
chron	chronological
C.H.U.D.	cannibalistic humanoid underground dwellers (cult horror movie)
chunder	watch under! (Australian warning that someone is throwing up)
CI	Channel Islands
CIA	Central Intelligence Agency (US)
CIB	Criminal Investigation Branch
CICB	Criminal Injuries Compensation Board
CID	Criminal Investigation Department
Cie	*Compagnie*: French company (as in *Bracquart et Cie*)
C-in-C	Commander-in-Chief
CIP	Common Industrial Policy; cataloguing in publication data
circ	circulation (of publications); circular
cit	citation; cited
CIVB	Conseil Interprofessionnel du Vin de Bordeaux
CJD	Creutzfeldt-Jakob disease
CKD	completely knocked down (of disassembled cars, products, etc)
cl	centilitre; class; cloth (bookbinding)
Cllr	Councillor

clr	clear
cm	centimetre; **cm2** = square centimetre; **cm3** = cubic centimetre
Cmdr	Commander
Cmdre	Commodore
CMG	Companion of St Michael and St George
CND	Campaign for Nuclear Disarmament
CNR	Canadian National Railway
Co, co	company; county
c/o	in the care of; cash order
CO	Commanding Officer; Central Office
cob	close of business
COBOL	Computer Business Oriented Language
COD	cash/collect on delivery
CODOT	Classification of occupations and directory of occupational titles
COED	computer operated electronic display; *Concise Oxford English Dictionary*
co-ed	co-educational
CofA	Certificate of Airworthiness
CofE	Church of England
COI	Central Office of Information
Col	Colonel
coll	collection; college; colloquialism
Comdr	Commander
Comdt	Commandant
COMECON	Council for Mutual Economic Assistance (EU)
COMPAC	Commonwealth Trans-Pacific Telephone Cable
compo	plastering composition; compensation
conc	concentrated
cond	condition; conduct
condo	condominium
confed	confederation; confederate
Cons, cons	Conservative; Consul; constitution
consols	consolidated annuities (Government securities)
cont	continued

Co-Op	Co-operative society or union
COPAT	Council for the Prevention of Art Theft (columnist Fritz Speigl has waggishly suggested, "Why not *Worldwide* Prevention?")
COPS	Cognitive Profiling System
CORE	Congress of Racial Equality (US)
Corp, corp	Corporation
corr	correction; correspondent
COSLA	Convention of Scottish Local Authorities
CO2	carbon dioxide gas
COTS	Childlessness Overcome Through Surrogacy
COW	Cow Observers Worldwide (group of cow enthusiasts which publishes a quarterly 'Moosletter')
CP	Common Prayer; Communist Party; Country Party (Australia); Court of Probate
cp	compare
CPA	Canadian Pacific Airlines; certified public accountant (US)
CPI	consumer price index
Cpl	Corporal
CPLP	Community of Portuguese Speaking Countries
CPR	cardiopulmonary resuscitation
CPRE	Council for the Protection of Rural England
CPRW	Council for the Protection of Rural Wales
CPU	central processing unit (computers)
CRAFT Club	'Can't Remember a Flippin' Thing' Club
CRE	Commission for Racial Equality
Cres, cres	crescent

Creep

The American philologist William Safire tells an amusing story against himself when, during the Presidential campaign of 1972, he was asked to check the name of the Committee to Re-elect the President – at the time, President Nixon. Safire ran through a range of acronymous possibilities – **CTRTP, Comrep, Cre-Pres** and so on, and gave the name a clean bill of health. Unfortunately, he missed one; the Committee later became famous (or infamous) as **CREEP**. At about the same time an equally inapt acronym popped up for the internationally supported Law of the Sea Treaty, forever after to be known as **LOST**.

CRO	Criminal Records Office
CRS	Chinese restaurant syndrome (allegedly due to over-use of the flavour enhancer monosodium glutamate)
CSA	Child Support Agency
CSC	Civil Service Commission
CSE	Certificate of Secondary Education
CS gas	ortho-chlorobenzal malononitrile; named after the originators, Ben Carson and Roger Staughton
CSI	Chartered Surveyors' Institution
CSIRO	Commonwealth Scientific and Industrial Research Organisation
CSM	Company Sergeant-Major
CSO	Central Statistical Office
CSR	Colonial Sugar Refining Company (Aust)
CST	Central Standard Time
Ct	Carat (unit of weight for precious stones, pearls, gold alloys etc) *See also* **Kt** (karat) in the US
CTC	carbon tetrachloride (fire retardant)
CTN	confectioner, tobacconist and newsagent's shop
CTO	cancelled to order (philately)
CTR	control traffic zone (airports)
Ctrl	the modifier key on a computer
CTT	capital transfer tax
CTV	Canadian Television Network
cu cm	cubic centimetre (also **cu m** = cubic metre; **cu in** = cubic inch; **cu ft** = cubic foot; **cu yd** = cubic yard)
CUNY	City University of New York
CUP	Cambridge University Press

CURE	Care, Understanding, Research organisation for the welfarE of drug addicts
CV, cv	curriculum vitae: a summary of a person's career and attainments
CW	common wisdom
CWA	Civil Works Administration (US); Country Women's Association (Australia)
CWL	Catholic Women's League
cwo	cash with order
cwt	hundredweight (112 lbs)
cyl	cylinder
Cz	Czechoslovakia

D

They're all Damn Madd!

MADD (Mothers Against Drunk Driving) is a real organisation in the US, but its members were far from amused when a newspaper columnist riposted with DAMM – Drunks Against Mad Mothers. And organisations concerned with children and adults with learning disabilities weren't too pleased either when some wag suggested that the acronym for Mothers Against Dyslexia should be **DAM**.

D	Roman numeral for 500; Gambian dalasi (currency); December; Democrat, Democratic (US); demy (paper size); *Deus* = God; *Deutschland* = Germany; Devonian (geology); diameter; dinar; Vietnamese dong (currency); occupational category; *Dominus* = Lord; Dom; Don; *douane* = French customs; Duchess; Duke; Dutch
d	day; date; dam (animal pedigrees); daughter; dead; deceased; decree; degree; delete; deliver; delivery; density; *denarius* = old British pence (1d, 2d, 9d etc); depart; departure; depth; desert; diameter; died; dinar; discharged; distance; dividend; dose; drachma
DA	District Attorney (US); Department of Agriculture (US); deputy assistant; Algerian dinar; Diploma in Anaesthetics; Diploma in Art; dopamine

D/A	deposit account; days after acceptance; delivery on acceptance; digital to analogue (also **D-A**)
DAB	digital audio broadcasting; Dictionary of American Biography
DAD	deputy assistant director
DAF, daf	*Doorn Automobielfabriek* = Dutch car manufacturer
daffs	daffodils
DAGrSc	Doctor of Agricultural Science
DAI, dai	death from accidental injuries
Dan	Danish
Dan-Air	Davies and Newman Ltd (British airline)
D&B	Dun and Bradstreet (US financial reports); discipline and bondage
D&C, d&c	dilation and curettage; dean and chapter
d&d	drunk and disorderly; death and dying
D&V	diarrhoea and vomiting
dap	documents against payment; do anything possible
DAR	Daughters of the American Republic (US)
DARE	demand and resource evaluation
DAS	Dramatic Authors' Society
DASc	Doctor of Agricultural Science
DAT	digital audio tape; digital analogue technology; dementia of the Alzheimer type
DATA	Draughtsmen's and Allied Technicians' Association
DATV	digitally assisted television
DAX	*Deutche Aktien-index* = German price share index
dB, db	decibel
DB	Bachelor of Divinity; delayed broadcast; Deutsche Bundesbank; Deutsche Bundesbahn (German railways); double-barrelled
DBH	diameter at breast height (forestry)
Dbn	Durban, South Africa
DBS	direct broadcast by satellite
DC	Distict of Columbia (as in Washington, DC); death certificate; Deputy Commissioner; Detective Constable; direct current; District Commissioner;

	Douglas Commercial (US aircraft series, eg DC3, DC10, etc); documents against cash
dc	dead centre; double column (printing); direct current; drift correction
DCA	Department of Civil Aviation (Australia)
DCM	Distinguished Conduct Medal
D&C	dilation and curettage (uterus operation)
d col	double column (publishing)
DD	Doctor of Divinity
d&d	drunk and disorderly
DDA	Disabled Drivers' Association
D-day	Start of Allied invasion of mainland Europe, WW2
DDG	deputy director general
DDR	*Deutsche Demokratische Republik* (formerly East Germany)
DDS	Dewey Decimal System (library classification); Doctor of Dental Surgery
DDT	dichloro-diphenyl-trichloroethane (insecticide)
Dec	December
dec	deceased; decimal; decrease
def	definition; definitive; defect; deficit
del	*delineavit* = drawn by (on engravings); delegate
deli	delicatessen

DELTA   DON'T EXPECT LUGGAGE
        TO ARRIVE

DELTA	don't expect luggage to arrive (*qv Airline Acronyms*)

demo	demonstration
Den	Denmark
dep	depart; departure; depot; deposit
Dept, dept	department
der	derivative; derivation
derv	diesel engined road vehicle
DES	Department of Education and Science
DET	diethyltryptamine (hallucinogenic drug)
Det, det	Detective; detached
DEWLINE	distant early warning viewing line (US defence)
DF	Defender of the Faith
DFC	Distinguished Flying Cross
DFM	Distinguished Flying Medal
DG, D-G	director-general
DHA	District Health Authority
DHSS	former Department of Health and Social Security (now split into **DoH** and **DSS**)
DI	Detective Inspector; donor insemination
diag	diagonal; diagram
diam	diameter
dib, dib, dib	*See* **dyb, dyb, dyb**
DIC	drunk in charge (police term)
dil	dilute
DIN	*Deutsche Industrie fur Normen* (measurement of speed of photographic film)
DINKY	double income, no kids yet
Dip, dip	diploma (also **dipl**)
DipAD	Diploma in Art and Design
DipCom	Diploma of Commerce
DipEd	Diploma of Education
Dir, dir	director
dis	district; distinguished; distance
div	division
DIY, diy	do it yourself
DJ, dj	dinner jacket; disc jockey
DLitt	Doctor of Letters; Doctor of Literature

DLO	Dead Letter Office
DLP	former Democratic Labor Party (Australia)
dlr	dealer
DM	Deutschmark
DMS	data management system; Diploma of Management Studies
DMT	dimethyltryptamine (hallucinogenic drug)
DMus	Doctor of Music
DMZ	demilitarised zone
DNA	deoxyribonucleic acid, the main constituent of chromosomes
DNB	*Dictionary of National Biography*
D-notice	Government restriction warning prohibiting publication of information considered vital to national security
DNS	Department for National Savings
DOA	dead on arrival
DOCG	*Denominazione di Origine Controllata Garantita*: Italian guarantee that wine is from the district named on the label

Doctors' Abbreviations

In Britain patients are legally entitled to see their medical casenotes. But if you did peek at your doctor's scrawl, peppered with arcane slang and medical abbreviations, would you understand it even it if was legible? You would have cause for alarm if you spotted **Review SOS**, but in fact SOS here is short for the Latin *sid opus sit*: if symptoms persist. On the other hand the letters **DNR** effectively disguise a truly grim reality: do not resuscitate. Other common abbreviations include **VMI** (very much improved) and **NAD** (nothing abnormal detected).

More common are the 'gallows humour' acronyms known to all medical students and young doctors, like **GORK** (God only really knows!) and **ADT** on a prescription (any damn thing!). Then there are **LOL in NAD** (little old lady in no apparent distress); **CC** (chief complaint); **YoYo**, the sign-off for discharged patients (you're on your own!) and the ghoulish **GPO** (good for parts only); **MFC** (measure for coffin) and **ECU** (eternal care unit, ie, morgue). **FLK** on a child's notes means 'funny looking kid', while **GRINED** means 'Guardian reader in ethnic dress.'

DOD	Department of Defense (US)
DOE	Department of the Environment
DOM	*Deo Optimo Maximo*: Latin for 'God is best and greatest', the motto of the Benedictine Order and seen on the labels of Benedictine liqueur; dirty old man
DORA	Defence of the Realm Act, enacted during World War 1 to enforce security restrictions
dorm	dormitory
DOS	disc (or disk) operating system, as in MS-DOS and PC-DOS
doz	dozen
DP	displaced person; data processing
DPh	Doctor of Philosophy
DPM	Deputy Prime Minister; Diploma of Psychological Medicine
DPP	Director of Public Prosecutions
DPW	Department of Public Works
Dr	doctor
dr	debit; debtor; drachm; drachma; drawn; drive
D-RAM	dynamic random access memory
DSC	Distinguished Service Cross
DSc	Doctor of Science
DSM	Distinguished Service Medal
DSO	Distinguished Service Order
DSS	Department of Social Security
DST	daylight saving time
dstn	destination
DTI	Department of Trade and Industry
DTP	desktop publishing

DTs	delirium tremens
dub	dubious
dup	duplicate
Dur	Durham
DV	Domestic Violence Division, Scotland Yard
DVD	digital video disc; **DVD-Rom** = recordable DVD
DVLC	Driver and Vehicle Licensing Centre, Swansea
DVM	Doctor of Veterinary Medicine
d/w	dust wrapper; also **d/j** = dust jacket (books)
D/W	deadweight
DWD	driving while disqualified
DWI	Dutch West Indies
dwt	pennyweight (one twentieth of an ounce)
DX	Telecom symbol for long distance; deep six (to 'deep six' something is to bury it, literally or figuratively)
dyb	Do Your Best (Scout's motto). Hence the traditional Cubs' call, "dyb, dyb, dyb!"
Dylan	Dynamic LANguage, an Apple computer programming language

DRAG   DIMINISH RELIANCE ON ACRONYMS GENERALLY

East, West and other Points of the Compass

Starting with *north* and moving clockwise: **N** (north); **NNE** (north-northeast); **NE** (northeast); **ENE** (east-northeast); **E** (east); **ESE** (east-southeast); **SE** (southeast); **SSE** (south-southeast); **S** (south); **SSW** (south-southwest); **SW** (southwest); **WSW** (west-southwest); **W** (west); **WNW** (west-northwest); **NW** (northwest) and **NNW** (north-northwest).

E	Earl; earth (planet); earth (electric circuit); East; eastern; postcode for East London; Easter; ecstasy (drug); elliptical galaxy (astronomy); England; English; E-number (see detailed entry); energy; equator; lowest occupational category; equator; evening; evensong; electromotive force (physics); *Espana* = Spain; second-class merchant ship (Lloyd's Register)
e	edition; eldest; electric; electricity; electromotive; electron; engineer; Erlang (telecommunications unit); error (baseball); evening; excellent; excellence; transcendental number (mathematics)
EA	East Anglia; educational age; electrical artificer; *Ente Autonomo* = Autonomous Corporation (Italy); environmental assessment
ea	each

41

EAA	Edinburgh Architectural Association
EAAA	European Association of Advertising Agencies
EAC	East African Community; Educational Advisory Committee; Engineering Advisory Council
EACSO	East African Common Services Organisation
E&OE	errors and omissions excepted
EAON, eaon	except as otherwise noted
EAP	English for academic purposes; Edgar Allan Poe (US author)
EAR	employee attitude research
EAS	equivalent air speed
EAT	earliest arrival time (also **eat**); Employment Appeal Tribunal
EAX	electronic automated exchange (telecommunications)
EB	Encyclopaedia Britannica; electricity board; electronic beam
EBA	English Bowling Association
EBC	European Billiards Confederation; European Brewery Convention
EBL	European Bridge League
EBM	expressed breast milk
EBU	European Boxing Union; European Badminton Union; European Broadcasting Union; English Bridge Union
EBV	Epstein-Barr virus
EC	European Community (now **EU**, European Union); postcode for East Central London; East Caribbean; Episcopal Church
ec	earth closet; enamel coated; *exempli causa* = for example
ECA	Electrical Contractors' Association
ecc	*eccetera* = etc (Italy)
ECD	early closing day; estimated completion date
ECG	electrocardiogram; electrocardiograph; export credit guarantee

ECHO virus	Enteric Cytopathic Human Orphan virus (also **echovirus**)
ECM	European Common Market (now **EU**, qv)
ECO	English Chamber Orchestra
ECS	European Communications Satellite
ECSC	European Coal and Steel Community
ECU	English Church Union; extra close-up (film and TV)
ecu	European currency unit
ed	editor; edition; edited
EDC	European Defence Community
Edin	Edinburgh
EDM	electronic distance measurement (surveying)
EDP, edp	electronic data processing
EDSAT	Educational Television Satellite
EDT	Eastern Daylight Time
EDTA	ethylenediaminetetra-acetic acid (bleach stabiliser in detergents)
ee	errors excepted
EEC	European Economic Community (now **EU**)
EEG	electroencephalogram; electrocncephalograph
EENT	eye, ear, nose and throat (medical specialism). *qv* **ENT**
EET	Eastern European Time
EETPU	Electrical, Electronic, Telecommunications and Plumbing Union
EFL	English as a foreign language
EFTA	European Free Trade Association
EFTPOS	electronic funds transfer at point of sale
EFTS	electronic funds transfer system
eg	*exempli gratia* = for example
EGM	extraordinary general meeting
EGU	English Golf Union
EHF	European Hockey Federation; extremely high frequency
EHO	environmental health officer

EIS	Educational Institute of Scotland
EL	easy listening (radio format)
el	elevated railroad (US); electrical
El Al	Israeli Airlines
E-layer	lower layer of ionised gases in the earth's ionosphere that reflects radio waves. aka Heaviside layer
elev	elevation
ELF	Eritrean Liberation Front; extremely low frequency
Eliz	Elizabeth; Elizabethan
ELT	English language teaching
ELU	English Lacrosse Union
E-mail	electronic mail
emer	emergency; emeritus
EMI	Electric and Musical Industries Limited
Emma	Emmanuel College, Oxford
Emp	Emperor; Empress; Empire
EMS	European monetary system
EMU	European monetary unit; economic and monetary union; electromagnetic unit (also **emu**)
EN	enrolled nurse
encyc	encyclopaedia
ENEA	European Nuclear Energy Agency
ENG	electronic news gathering
Eng	England; English
eng	engine; engineer
engr	engraver; engraved
ENO	English National Opera
ENT	ear, nose and throat (medical speciality) *qv* **EENT**
env	envelope
EOC	Equal Opportunities Commission
EOKA	Cypriot Campaign for Union with Greece
EPC	Educational Publishers' Council
EPCOT	experimental prototype community of tomorrow (at Disney World, Florida)

E numbers

These are code numbers for natural and artificial additives to food and drink that have been accepted as safe throughout the European Community. Numbers without the E on product labels are additives approved by the UK but not yet by the EU. Some of the E numbers denote traditional natural additives such as E120 (red cochineal colouring), E140 (green chlorophyll), E406 (agar, used in icecream), E220 (sulphur dioxide, a preservative). Others are undoubtedly creations from the test tube, such as E233 (2-thiazol-4-yl benzimidazole thiabenzadole, used to treat bananas).

Here are some of the more common E numbers:

Colours

E100   curcumin – used in flour and margarine
E101   riboflavin
E102   The notorious tartrazine, used to heighten the orange colour of soft drinks and blamed by many for "driving hyperactive kids barmy".

E102

E104   quinoline yellow – used to colour smoked fish
E150   caramel
E153   vegetable carbon – used in liquorice

E162   beetroot red (betanin) – used in icecream
E171   titanium oxide – used in sweets
E174   silver (yes, the metal!) – used in cake decorations

Antioxidants

E300   L-ascorbic acid – used in fruit drinks and bread
E307   synthetic alpha-tocopherol – used in baby foods
E310   propyl gallate – chewing gum, vegetable oils
E320   butylated hydroxytoluene – soup mixes, cheese spreads

Preservatives

E200   sorbic acid – soft drinks, yogurt, cheese slices
E201   sodium sorbate
E202   potassium sorbate
E203   calcium sorbate – frozen pizzas, cakes, buns
E210   benzoic acid
E221   sodium sulphite
E227   calcium bisulphite – dried fruit and vegetables, fruit juices, sausages, dairy desserts, cider, beer and wine
E252   potassium nitrate – used for curing ham, bacon, corned beef, some cheese

Emulsifiers and stabilisers

E322   lecithins – chocolate and low fat spreads
E400   alginic acid – icecream, soft cheese
E407   carrageenan – milk shakes, jellies
E410   carob gum – salad cream
E412   guar gum – packet soups
E413   gum tragacanth – salad dressing, cheese
E414   gum arabic – confectionery
E440   pectin – jams and preserves
E465   ethylmethylcellulose – used in gateaux

Others

E420   sorbitol – diabetic jams and confectionery
E170   calcium carbonate
E260   acetic acid

E290	carbon dioxide – carbonates fizzy drinks
E330	citric acid
E334	tartaric acid
E338	orthophosphoric acid – flavourings

Be warned that non-E numbers on packaging include potentially harmful agents: 507 (hydrochloric acid), 513 (sulphuric acid), 536 (potassium ferrocyanide), 925 (chlorine). The frequently criticised flavour enhancer monosodium glutamate or MSG sometimes hides behind its code number, 621.

EPNS	electroplated nickel silver
EPOCH	End Physical Punishment of Children
EPOS	electronic point of sale
EPP	executive pension plan
eps	earnings per share
equiv	equivalent
ER	*Elizabeth Regina* = Queen Elizabeth; *Eduardus Rex* = King Edward
ERA	Education Reform Act
ERBM	extended range ballistic missile
ERG	electrical resistance gauge
ERGOM	European Research Group on Management
ERM	European Rate Mechanism
ERNIE	electronic random number indicator equipment (selects prizewinners from Premium Bond numbers)
ERS	earnings related supplement
ERU	English Rugby Union
ERV	English Revised Version of the Bible
E's	The elements that can cause angina: *exertion, emotion, eating, extremes* and *entercourse* (doctors can't spell)
ESA	Educational Supply Association; environmentally sensitive area

ESCAP	Economic and Social Commission for Asia and the Pacific
ESCO	Educational, Scientific and Cultural Organisation (UN)
ESG	English standard gauge
ESL	English as a second language
ESN	educationally subnormal (60-80 IQ)
ESP	English for special purposes; extra-sensory perception
esp	especially
esq	esquire
ESRO	European Space Research Organisation
ESSO	Standard Oil Company
est	established; estate; estimated; estuary
EST	Eastern Standard Time; electric shock treatment
ESU	English Speaking Union; electrostatic unit
ETA	estimated time of arrival
et al	*et alii* = and others; *et alibi* = and elsewhere
etc	*et cetera* = and so on
ETD	estimated time of departure
ETF	electronic transfer of funds
et seq	*et sequens* = and the following; *et sequentia* = and those that follow
etym; etymol	etymology; etymological
EU	European Union; Evangelical Union
EVA	extra vehicular activity (outside a spacecraft)
evg, evng	evening
EWO	educational welfare officer
ex, exc	excellent; excess; excursion; exempt; excluding; former (as in ex-Army, ex-husband etc)
Exc	Excellency
exch	exchange
excl	exclusive; excluding
ex div	ex dividend
exec	executor; executive

exes	expenses
exhib	exhibit; exhibitor
ex int	ex interest
Exon	Bishop of Exeter
exp	expense; expenses; experience; experiment; export; express
expo	large-scale exposition or exhibition
expurg	expurgate
ext	extension; exterior; external; extra; extinct

F

We're all jolly good Fellows!

The letters **FIMechE** following a person's name means that he or she is a Fellow of the Institute of Mechanical Engineers. Worldwide, there are millions of Fellows belonging to hundreds of Institutes – **FInstPC**, for example, is a Fellow of the Institute of Public Cleansing – so when you see an abbreviation beginning with **FI** or **FR** there is a good chance that it refers to a Fellow of some learned, professional or trade body. But you can be fooled. There are a lot of FIs which are abbreviations of the French *Federation internationale*, such as **FIFA**, which in English is the International Association Football Federation. Other traps include **FID** (Falkland Islands Dependencies), **FICA** (Federal Insurance Contributions Act in the US), **FIFO** (first in, first out), **FEA** (Federation of European Aerosol Associations), **FGA** (Flat Glass Association) and **FPA** (Family Planning Association). And take care if a name has the attached abbreviation **FRCS**. It could be that the holder is an esteemed Fellow of the Royal College of Surgeons or, on the other hand (if you're in Australia) a member of the Federation of Rabbit Clearance Societies. The most important Institutes are listed in the dictionary.

F
Fahrenheit; family; farad; father; fathom; February; Federation; Fellow; feminine; fiction; filly; fine (metallurgy, numismatics); fog; folio; foolscap (paper size); foul; franc; francs; *Frauen* =

	woman; France; French; *Frère* = Brother; Friday; US fighter aircraft series (**F-111** etc); filial generation (genetic; **F1, F2** etc)
f	face value (numismatics, philately); fair; father; fathom; feet (also **ft**); female; feminine; filly; fine; f-number (photographic focal length/aperture ratio, eg **F6**); following; *forte* = loudly; formula; folio; foul; fog; founded; franc; freehold; frequency; furlong; Dutch guilder
FA	Football Association; fatty acid; filtered air; fire alarm; Finance Act; folic acid; furnace annealed; Fanny Adams (euphemism for *fuck all*)
FAA	Federal Aviation Aministration (US); Fellow Australian Academy of Science; Film Artists' Association; Fleet Air Arm; free amino acid
FAAAS	Fellow of the American Academy of Arts and Sciences
fab	fabric
fabbr	*fabbrica* = factory
Fab Soc	Fabian Society
FACS	Fellow of the American College of Surgeons
fac	facsimile (qv **FAX, fax**)
FACT	Federation Against Copyright Theft
fad	free air delivered
Faer	Faeroe Islands
FA Cup	Football Association Cup, open to all teams of the Association
Fahr	Fahrenheit (also **Fah, fahr**)
FAI	*Federation aeronautique internationale* = International Aeronautical Federation
FAIA	Fellow of the Association of International Accountants
Falk I	Falkland Islands
FALN	*Fuerzas Armadas de Liberacion Nacional* = Armed Forces of National Liberation (Puerto Rico)

fam	family; familiar
FANY	First Aid Nursing Yeomanry
f&a	fore and aft
f&d	freight and demurrage
f&f	fixtures and fittings
fam	family; familiar
f&t	fire and theft
FAO	Food and Agriculture Organisation (UN)
fao	for the attention of; finished all over
faq	fair average quality; free alongside quay
FAR	free for accident reported (no claim on insurance)
FASA	Fellow of the Australian Society of Accountants
FAST	factor analysis system
fath	fathom
fav	favourite
FAX, fax	facsmile transmission; facsimile equipment
FB	fire brigade; fisheries board; Forth Bridge; Free Baptist
F-B	full-bore (guns)
fb	fullback (football)
FBA	Fellow of the British Academy
FC	Forestry Commission
fcp	foolscap (paper size)
FCC	Federal Communications Commission (US)
FCCA	Fellow of the Chartered Association of Certified Accountants
FCI	International Federation of Kennel Clubs
FCII	Fellow of the Chartered Insurance Institute
FCO	Foreign and Commonwealth Office
FD	*Fidei Defensor* = Defender of the Faith
fd	forward; found; founded
FDA	Food and Drug Administration (US)
FDC	first day cover (philately)
FDR	Franklin Delano Roosevelt, former US president
fdr	founder

Feb	February
fec	*fecit* = made by (on antique prints and engravings)
Fed	Federal; Federal Reserve Bank (US)
fem	female; feminine
FES	foil, epee and sabre
Fest, fest	festival
FF	Fianna Fail (Irish polical party)
ff	folios; fixed focus
FG	Fine Gael (Irish political party)
F/H, f/h	freehold (also **fhold** and **fhld**)
FHA	Federal Housing Administration (US)
FHB	'family hold back' (warning to children not to eat before the guests)
FIA	Fellow of the Institute of Actuaries
FIAT	*Fabbrica Italiana Automobili Torina*, Turin car makers
fict	fiction (also **fic**)
FICA	Federal Insurance Contributions Act (US)
Fid Def	*Fidei Defensor* (*qv* FD)
FIDE	*Federation Internationale des Echecs* = International Chess Federation
FIDO	Federation of Irate Dog Owners; dedicated to the reform of Britain's animal quarantine laws (*qv* PFP)
FIFA	*Federation Internationale de Football Association* = International Association Football Federation; International Federation of Art Film Makers
FIFO	first in, first out
15 cert	British Board of Film Censors classification for films not suitable for children under 15
fig	figure
FIH	*Federation Internationale de Hockey* – International Hockey Federation
FILO	first in, last out
FIM	*Federation Internationale Motocycliste* = International Motorcyclists' Federation

fin	*finis* = the end; final; financial
FINA	*Federation internationale de natation amateur* = International Amateur Swimming Federation
Findus	Fruit INDUStries Limited
fix	fixture
FLAK	fondest love and kisses
Flak	*Fliegerabwehrkanone* = anti-aircraft fire or artillery; now means a quantity of adverse criticism
FLAME	Fight Linkroads And M25 Expansion
fld	filed
fldg	folding
FLN	*Front de Liberation Nationale* = National Liberation Front of Algeria
fl	floor; fluid; guilder (in the Netherlands)
fl oz	fluid ounces
flrg	flooring
FM	frequency modulation
fm	farm
FMCG	fast moving consumer goods
fmr	former; farmer
FNMA	Federal National Mortgage Association (US), fondly known as 'Fannie Mae'
FMV	full motion video
FO	Foreign Office; Flying Officer (also **F/O**)
FOAF	friend of a friend
FOB, fob	free on board
FoC, foc	father of the chapel (print unions)
fo'c's'le	forecastle (on a ship)
FoE, FOE	Friends of the Earth
FOH	front of house (theatres)
fol	folio; following
F-111	Famous swing-wing US fighter-bomber launched in 1968
Footsie	*see* FT-SE 100
FOR	free on rail

FOREST   FREEDOM ORGANISATION FOR THE RIGHT
TO ENJOY SMOKING TOBACCO

FOREST	Freedom Organisation for the Right to Enjoy Smoking Tobacco
FORTRAN	FORmula TRANslation: computer programming language
The 48	Bach's two books of preludes and fugues for clavier
4WD	four wheel drive
FP, fp	fireplace; fresh paragraph; fully paid; freezing point
FPA	Family Planning Association
FPO	field post office (Army)
FPS	Fellow of the Pharmaceutical/Philosophical/Physical Society
fps	frames per second; feet per second
fr	franc (sometimes Ffr for French franc, etc); front; from; frequent; fruit; father
FRAME	Fund for the Replacement of Animals in Medical Experiments
FRCM	Fellow of the Royal College of Music
FRCP	Fellow of the Royal College of Physicians
FRCS	Fellow of the Royal College of Surgeons
FRCVS	Fellow of the Royal College of Veterinary Surgeons
FRED	Fast Reactor Experiment, Dounreay, Scotland
FRG	Federal Republic of Germany (formerly West Germany)

FRGS	Fellow of the Royal Geographical Society
Fri	Friday
FRICS	Fellow of the Institute of Chartered Surveyors
front	frontispiece (also **frontis**)
FT	*Financial Times*, London. *qv* FT Index, FT-SE 100, Footsie
ft	foot; feet. **sq ft** = square foot/feet; **cu ft** = cubic foot/feet
FTC	Federal Trade Commission (US)
FT Index	*Financial Times* industrial ordinary share index
FTP	file transfer protocol
FT-SE 100	*Financial Times* Stock Exchange 100-share index (Footsie)
FU	Farmers' Union
fur	furlong
FWA	Federal Works Agency (US)
FWD, fwd	forward; front wheel drive; four wheel drive
fyi	for your information
FZS	Fellow of the Zoological Society

ABQUIZ

Although all the abbreviations in this dictionary are spelt without periods, their meanings are invariably clear. Confusion arises, however, when necessary spacing between the elements of an abbreviation is also banished. For example:

1 **POBOX11**	2 **VOLIV**	3 **FLOZ**
4 **PROMOMA**	5 **DOOGO**	6 **NO1O**

Written out in full, these are: 1. P.O. Box 11 2. Volume Four 3. fluid ounces 4. Public Relations Officer, Museum of Modern Art 5. Director of Operations, Orbiting Geophysical Observatory (US) 6. No.10 (Downing Street)

G

G	General Exhibition (film censor category in some countries); German; Germany; Gibbs function (thermodynamics); good; Haitian gourde (currency); grand (slang for $1,000); grey; green; Guernsey; Gulf; Paraguayan guarani (currency)
g	gallon; gale; garage; gas; gaseous; gauge; gelding; gender; general; gilt; goal; goalkeeper; gold; gram; gravity; great; green; grey; guardian; guilder; guilders; guinea; guineas
GA	General Assembly (UN); General American (language); Geographical Association; Geologists' Association; general anaesthetic; graphic arts
G/A, g/a	ground to air (missiles); general average (also **GA, ga**)
GAA	Gaelic Athletic Association
Gabba	Wollongabba (Queensland Cricket Club ground in Brisbane)
GAC	granular activated carbon
Gael	Gaelic
GAFTA	Grain and Free Trade Association
Gal	Galway, Ireland
gal	gallon (also **gall**)
GALAXY	General Automatic Luminosity high-speed scanner at the Royal Observatory, Edinburgh
galv	galvanised; galvanic; galvanometer

GAM	guided aircraft missile
Gam	The Gambia
G&AE	general and administration expenses
G&O	gas and oxygen (anaesthesia)
G&S	Gilbert and Sullivan
G&T	gin and tonic
GAO	*Glovaya Astronomicheskaya Observatoriya* = Russia's central observatory
GAP	Great American Public
GAPAN	Guild of Air Pilots and Air Navigators
GAPCE	General Assembly of the Presbyterian Church of England
gar	garage; garden (also **gard**); garrison
GAR	guided aircraft rocket
GARP	Global Atmospheric Research Programme
GASP	Group Against Smog Pollution; Group Against Steroid Prescription
gastro	gastroenteritis; gastroenterology (also **gastroent**)
GATCO	Guild of Air Traffic Control Officers
GATT	General Agreement on Tariffs and Trade (also **Gatt**)
GAUFCC	General Assembly of Unitarian and Free Christian Churches
GAV	gross annual value
GAW	gross annual wage

Gay

An abbreviation or a purloined adjective? Whatever the truth, here's a word that has acquired a considerable mythology in just a few decades. There's a strong claim that the word's use as a description of a homosexual person derives from New York's 1969 Stonewall rally during which banners proclaimed that the marchers were as 'Good As You', hence the acronym. On the other hand, usage of the word **gay** in this context can be traced to late 19th century literature, although it did not become popular until the 1960s when it quickly demolished traditional usage, as in, for example, 'gay blade', 'gay occasion' and so on.

GAYE	give as you earn (scheme to deduct charitable contributions from employees' pay packets)
gaz	gazette; gazetted
GB	Great Britain; gigabyte
GBE	Grand Cross of the British Empire
GBH	grievous bodily harm
GBS	Dramatist George Bernard Shaw
GC	George Cross (gallantry award)
GCA	ground control approach (airports)
GCB	Grand Cross of the Most Honourable Order of the Bath
GCE	General Certificate of Education
GCHQ	Government Communications Headquarters
GCM	Good Conduct Medal; General Court Martial
GCMG	Grand Cross of the Order of St Michael and St George
GCSE	General Certificate of Secondary Education
GCVO	Grand Cross of the Royal Victorian Order
gd	good
GDBA	Guide Dogs for the Blind Association
gdn, gdns	garden; gardens
GDR	German Democratic Republic (former East Germany)
GE	General Electric Co (US)
ge	gilt edge (books)
GEC	General Electric Corporation
GEMS	Global Environmental Monitoring System
Gen	General
gen	gender; general; generic; genuine
gent	gentleman; **Gents** = men's lavatory
geog	geography; geographical
GEOREF	International Geographic Reference System
GESTAPO	*GEheime STAats-POlizei*, former German secret police
G5	Group of Five (France, Japan, US, Germany and UK as a currency stabilising group)

GF	General Foods
GFR	German Federal Republic (formerly West Germany)
GFS	Girls' Friendly Society
GG	Grenadier Guards
GGA	former Girl Guides' Association
GHQ	general headquarters
gi	galvanised iron
GI	Government Issue (term for US soldier, WW2)
Gib	Gibraltar
GIFT	gamete intra-fallopian transfer (fertilisation technique)
GIGO	garbage in, garbage out (computer term)
GKN	Guest, Keen & Nettlefold's (engineering)
Gk	Greek
gl	glass; gloss
glad, gladdie	gladiolus; also Gladys Moncrieff, former Australian soprano (d.1976) known as 'Our Glad'
Glam	Glamorgan
GLASS	Gay and Lesbian Assembly for Student Support (US)
GLC	Greater London Council
gld	guilder
GLOMEX	Global Oceanographic and Meteorological Experiment
Glos	Gloucestershire
GM	General Motors Corporation; George Medal; general manager; genetically modified
gm	gram
G-man	Officer of the Federal Bureau of Investigation (Government man)
GMB	Grand Master of the Order of the Bath; General, Municipal and Boilermakers' Union
GMBE	Grand Master of the Order of the British Empire
GmbH	*Gesellschaft mit beschrankter Haftung*, a limited liability company in Germany

GMC	General Medical Council
GMDSS	Global Maritime Distress and Safety System, which replaced morse code in February, 1999
GMT	Greenwich Mean Time
GMWU	National Union of General and Municipal Workers
gn, gns	guinea; guineas
gnd	ground
GNP	gross national product
GOM	Grand Old Man (originally Prime Minister Gladstone) but today used to describe a senior and respected person
GOP	Grand Old Party (US Republican party); *Girls' Own Paper*
Gov	Governor
Gov-Gen	Governor-General
govt	government
GP	general practitioner (medical doctor); Grand Prix; general purpose
Gp Capt	Group Captain
gph	gallons per hour
GPI	general paralysis of the insane
GPO	general post office
GPS	Great Public Schools (Australia)
GPU	*Gosudarstevnnoye politicheskoye upravlenie* = former Soviet secret police
GQ	general quarters
Gr	Greek; Grecian
gr	gram; grain; gross; grand; group; grade
GRA	Greyhound Racing Association
grad	graduate; gradient
GRI	*Georgius Rex Imperator* = George, King and Emperor
grm	gram
gr wt	gross weight
GS	Geological Survey; gold standard; general secretary; general staff

G7	Group of Seven (economic policy coordinating committee of seven leading industrial nations, excluding the former USSR: Canada, France, Germany, Italy, Japan, UK and US)
G77	Group of Seventy Seven (the world's developing countries)
GSM	general sales manager; group sales manager
GSO	General Staff Officer
GSOH	good sense of humour
G-spot	Grafenberg spot (vaginal erogenous zone)
G-string	Brief garment covering pubic area
GT	*gran turismo* = luxury high-performance sports saloon
GTC	General Teaching Council (Scotland)
G10	Group of Ten: original 1961 committee of nations which established IMF drawing rights (Belgium, Canada, France, Italy, Japan, Netherlands, Sweden, UK, US and West Germany)
gtd	guaranteed
gte	gilt top edge (books)
GUI	graphical user interface
guar	guarantee; guaranteed
Gulag	*Glavnoye Upravleniye ispravitel'no-trudovykh LAGerei* = a group of Russian labour camps, the subject of Alexandr Solzhenitsyn's 1973 novel, *The Gulag Archipelago*
GUM	*Gosudarstvenni Universalni Magazin* = official Russian department store
GUS	Great Universal Stores (UK)
GUT	great unified theory
guv	guv'nor; governor (Cockney term which recognises that 'you're the boss')
GV	*Grande Vitesse* = fast French train
GVHD	graft versus host disease
gvt	government (also **govt**)

GWP	Government white paper
GWR	Great Western Railway
gym	gymnasium; gymnastics

An abbreviation too far?

COLL GRADS   *Fees Paid*   *fr $11,70*

INS ANAL TRNEES

Six or more months credits reqd. No exp reqd.

BELL Agency   485 5thAv (42-42St)

This classified ad appeared in a New York daily. What the advertiser was presumably looking for were graduate trainees for insurance analysis!

H

H	degree of hardness in pencils, eg **2H**, **3H** etc; Hamiltonian (physics); Harbour; hearts (cards); heroin; histamine receptor; horn (music); hospital; hour; hydrant
h	harbour; hard; hardness; heat; height (also **ht**); high; hit (ball sports); heavy; horse; hot; hour; house; hundred; husband
HA	hardy annual (horticulture); Hautes-Alps (French department); Health Authority; high altitude
ha	hectare
Ha	Hawaii, Hawaiian, Haiti
ha	*hoc anno* = in this year; high angle
HAA	hepatitis-associated antigen
HA&M	*Hymns Ancient and Modern* (first published 1861)
hab	habitat; habitation
hab corp	habeas corpus
HAC	high alumina cement; Honourable Artillery Company
had	hereinafter described
haem	haemoglobin; haemorrage
HAI	hospital acquired infection
Hak Soc	Hakluyt Society
hal	halogen

Hal Orch	Hallé Orchestra
Ham	Hamburg, Germany
Han	Hanoverian
H&C, h&c	hot and cold (water)
H&E	heredity and environment; *Health & Efficiency* (naturist journal)
h&t	hardened and tempered
H&W	Harland & Wolff, Belfast shipbuilders
hanky	handkerchief (also hankie)
ha'penny	halfpenny; **ha'p'orth** = halfpenny worth
HAS	Health Advisory Service
haz	hazard; hazardous
HB	hard black pencil
Hb	haemoglobin (also **hem**)
H-beam	H-cross-section steel girder or joist
H-bomb	hydrogen (thermonuclear) bomb
hbk	hardback (book)
hbr	harbour
HC	Headmasters' Conference; High Commissioner; High Court; health certificate; highly commended; *hors de concours* = not for competition; Hague Convention; house of correction
Hcap, hcp	handicap
HCB	House of Commons Bill
HCE	Recurring abbreviation in James Joyce's *Finnegans Wake*, being the initials of the main character, H C Earwicker
HCSA	Hospital Consultants' and Specialists' Association
hcw	hot and cold water (also **hc, h&c**)
hdbk	hardback; handbook
HDipEd	Higher Diploma in Education
hdle	hurdle
hdlg	handling; **hdlg chg** = handling charge
hdqrs	headquarters
HDV	heavy duty vehicle

HE	Her/His Excellency; His Eminence; high explosive
Heb	Hebrew; Hebraic
HEC	Health Education Council
HECTOR	Heated Experimental Carbon Thermal Oscillator Reactor
hem	haemoglobin (also **Hb**); haemorrhage
Her	Herefordshire
HERALD	Highly Enriched Reactor at Aldermaston, Berkshire
herb	herbarium; herbaceous; herbalist
HERMES	Heavy Element and Radioactive Material Electromagnetic Separator
HERO	Hot Experimental Reactor O-power
Herts	Hertfordshire
HET	heavy equipment transporter
het	heterosexual
hex	hexagon; hexagonal
HF	high frequency; hard firm pencil
hf	half; **hf cf** = half calf binding (books)
hgr	hangar
HG	Home Guard
HGH	human growth hormone
hgt	height
HGV	heavy goods vehicle
HH	His Holiness; His/Her Honour; heavy hydrogen
hh	hands (height measurement of horses)
hhd	hogshead
Hib	Hibernian
hi-fi	high fidelity
HIM	His/Her Imperial Majesty
Hind	Hindi; Hindu
hippo	hippopotamus
hist	historic; historical; historian
histol	histology; histologist
HIV	human immunodeficiency virus

HIV-P	human immunodeficiency virus - positive
HJ	*hic jacet* = here lies; *hic jacet sepultus* = here lies buried
HK	Hong Kong; House of Keys (Manx Parliament)
HKJ	Hashemite Kingdom of Jordan
HL	House of Lords
hl	hectolitre
HLA system	human leucocyte antigen system
HM	Her/His Majesty; harbour master
hm	headmaster; headmistress; hectometre
HMAS	Her/His Majesty's Australian Ship
HMC	Headmasters' Conference (also **HC**)
HMCS	Her/His Majesty's Canadian Ship
HMG	Her/His Majesty's Government
HMHS	Her/His Majesty's Hospital Ship
HMIS	Her/His Majesty's Inspector of Schools
HMIT	Her/His Majesty's Inspector of Taxes
HMP	Her/His Majesty's Prison
HMS	Her/His Majesty's Ship; Her/His Majesty's Service
HMSO	Her/His Majesty's Stationery Office
HMV	His Master's Voice
HNC	Higher National Certificate
HND	Higher National Diploma
HO	Home Office; head office
ho	house
HOC, hoc	held in charge
HoC	House of Commons (also **HC, HofC, HOC**)
HoD	head of department
HoL	House of Lords (also **HofL**)
hol	holiday; holidays
Holl	Holland
HOLLAND	hope our love lasts and never dies
homeo	homoeopathic
homo	homosexual
Hon	Honorary (ie **Hon Sec** = honorary secretary);

	Honourable (ie. the Hon Matilda Smythe)
hons	honours
hon sec	honorary secretary
HOPEFUL	hard-up old person expecting full useful life
hor	horizon; horizontal
horol	horology; horologist
hort	horticulture; horticulturalist
hosp	hospital
HOTOL	HOrizontal Take Off and Landing aircraft
HP	Houses of Parliament; hot pressed (paper manufacture)
hp	horsepower; hire purchase; high pressure
HP sauce	Houses of Parliament sauce
HPTA	Hire Purchase Trade Association
HQ, hq	headquarters
HR	House of Representatives (US)
hr	hour
HRE	Holy Roman Empire
HRH	Her/His Royal Highness
Hrn	*Herren* = gentlemen (plural of *Herr*)
HRT	hormone replacement therapy
HS	Home Secretary; high school (also **HSch**)
HSE	Health and Safety Executive
hse	house
HSH	His/Her Serene Highness
HST	high speed train
HSV	herpes simplex virus
ht	height; heat; high tension; half time
h/t	halftone (printing)
HTML	hypertext markup language (World-Wide Web)
htd	heated
http	hypertext transfer protocol
ht wkt	hit wicket (cricket)
Hung	Hungary
HURT	Help Untwist Rape Trauma

HVA	Health Visitors' Association
hvy	heavy
h/w	hot water; husband and wife
HWLB	high water, London Bridge
HWS, hws	hot water system
hwy	highway
hyb	hybrid (botany)
hyd	hydraulic; hydrate
hypo	sodium thiosulphate, formerly sodium hyposulphate (photography)
Hz	hertz (unit of frequency)

He helium

I

Ibid, idem, inf and other footnotes

Here are the meanings of some of those italicised footnote abbreviations we suspect are put there simply to puzzle us:

abr = abridged; **app** = appendix; **ca** or **circa** = about;
cf = compare; **esp** = especially; **et seq** = and the following;
f = and the following page; **ff** = and the following pages;
ibid = in the same place; **id** or **idem** = by the same (author);
inf = below; **loc cit** = in the place cited; **ms** = manuscript;
mss = manuscripts; **NB** = take note of; **nd** = no date;
op cit = in the work cited; **passim** = throughout; **pl** = plate;
pp = pages; **pub** = published; **qv** = which see; **ser** = series;
sup = above; **suppl** = supplement; **trans** = translated or translation;
vide = see; **viz** = namely

I	*Iesus* = Jesus; roman numeral for one; instananeous current (physics); *Imperator* = Emperor; *Imperatrix* = Empress; Imperial; Peruvian inti (currency); Independence; Independent; India; Institute; International; Ireland; Irish; Island; Isle; Italian
i	incisor (dentistry); intransitive; interest (banking)
IA	Indian Army; infected area; initial allowance (tax); Institute of Actuaries; intra-arterial

ia	immediately available; *in absentia* = while absent; indicated altitude
I/A	Isle of Anglesey
IAA	International Advertising Association
IAAA	Irish Amateur Athletic Association; Irish Association of Advertising Agencies
IAAF	International Amateur Athletic Federation
IAAS	Incorporated Association of Architects and Surveyors
IAB	Industrial Arbitration Board; Industrial Advisory Board
IACA	Independent Air Carriers' Association
IACP	International Association of Chiefs of Police; International Association of Computer Programmers
IAE	Institute of Automotive Engineers; Institute of Atomic Energy (US)
IAEA	International Atomic Energy Agency
IAF	Indian Air Force; International Astronautical Federation
IAM	Institute of Administrative Management
IAS	indicated air speed; Indian Administrative Service; instrument approach system (aeronautics); infrared absorbed spectroscopy
IASA	International Air Safety Association
IAT, iat	International Atomic Time; inside air temperature
IATA	International Air Transport Association
IBA	Independent Broadcasting Authority; Independent Bankers' Association; International Bar Association
IBID	international bibliographical description
ibid	*ibidem* = in the same place
IBM	International Business Machines; intercontinental ballistic missile
IBS	irritable bowel syndrome

IC	*Iesus Christus* = Jesus Christ; Imperial College of Science and Technology, London (also **ICS**); industrial court; information centre
ic	internal combustion; integrated circuit; identity card
i/c	in charge; **2i/c** = second in charge/command

i/c   in charge

ICA	Institute of Contemporary Arts, London; Institute of Chartered Accountants; ignition control additive; internal carotid artery
ICAA	Invalid Childrens' Aid Association
ICAI	Institute of Chartered Accoutants in Ireland
ICAN	International Commission for Air Navigation
ICAO	International Civil Aviation Organisation
ICBM	intercontinental ballistic missile
ICC	Imperial Cricket Conference; International Chamber of Commerce; International Correspondence Colleges
ICCF	International Corresponding Chess Federation
ICE	Institute of Chartered Engineers; Institution of Civil Engineers; International Cultural Exchange
ICEF	International Council for Educational Films
ICFTU	International Confederation of Free Trade Unions

IChemE	Institute of Chemical Engineers
ICI	Imperial Chemical Industries
ICIANZ	Imperial Chemical Industries, Australia and New Zealand
ICJ	International Court of Justice
ICN	International Council of Nurses
ICOM	International Council of Museums
ICPO	International Criminal Police Organisation, *aka* **Interpol**
ICS	Imperial College of Science and Technology, London; Indian Civil Service; International Correspondence School
ICSU	International Council of Scientific Unions
ICU	intensive care unit
ICY	International Cooperation Year (1965)
ID	identification (card); Institute of Directors
IDA	International Development Association; Industrial Diamond Association
IDB	illicit diamond buyer
IDD	iodine deficiency disorder
IDL	international date line

I = The International Community

Just about every activity known to man has been elevated to international status, and the **I** for *International* abbreviation has proliferated on a truly global scale. Witness the **ICBD** (International Council of Ballroom Dancing); **ICCAT** (International Commission for the Conservation of Atlantic Tunas); the **IFM** (International Falcon Movement); and this real whopper, the **IFCTUSETMSCT**, which stands for International Federation of Christian Trade Unions of Salaried Employees, Technicians, Managerial Staff and Commercial Travellers! International listings alone would easily fill a book this size so only the most important are included here.

IDP	integrated data processing
IE	Indo-European (languages)
ie	*id est* = that is
IEA	Institute of Economic Affairs; Institution of Engineers, Australia
IEE	Institution of Electrical Engineers
IF	intermediate frequency
IFA	independent financial advisor
IFJ	International Federation of Journalists
IFLA	International Federation of Library Associations
IFR	instrument flying regulations
IFTA	International Federation of Travel Agencies; International Federation of Teachers' Associations
IG	inspector general
IGF	International Gymnastic Federation
IGM	International Grandmaster (chess)
IGWF	International Garment Workers' Federation

IKEA

IGY	International Geophysical Year (1957-8)
IHF	International Hockey Federation
IHRB	International Hockey Rules Board
II	Roman numeral for two (2)
III	Roman numeral for three (3); Investment in Industry organisation
IKEA	Initials of Ingrar Kamprad, founder of the retail furniture chain, and his home 'Elmtaryd' in Agunnaryd, Sweden
ILC	International Law Commission
ILEA	Inner London Education Authority
ILGA	Institute of Local Government Administration
ILGWU	International Ladies' Garment Workers' Union
ill	illustration; illustrated
ILO	International Labour Organisation
ILR	independent local radio
ILS	instrument landing system
IM	International Master (chess)
IMarE	Institute of Marine Engineers
IMCO	Intergovernmental Maritime Consultative Organisation
IMechE	Institution of Mechanical Engineers
IMinE	Institution of Mining Engineers
IMF	International Monetary Fund; International Motorcycle Federation
imp	impression (printing); imperial; imported
IMPACT	implementation planning and control technique
imperf	imperforate (philately)
in	inch; in^2 = square inch; in^3 = cubic inch
IN	Indian Navy
Inc, inc	incorporated; income
INCB	International Narcotics Control Board
incl	include; included; including; inclusive; incline
IND	*in nomine Dei* = in the name of God

IN THE NAME OF GOD, I COME

IN THE NAME OF INDIAN, YOU GO

IND in nomine Dei in the name of God
ind Indian

Ind	India; Indian
ind	independent; index; indirect; industry; industrial
indef	indefinite
indic	indicator; indicative
indie	independent recording or film production company
inf	information (also **info**); infantry; inferior
infl	influence; influenced
infra dig	*infra dignitatem* = undignified; beneath one's dignity
init	initial
INLA	Irish National Liberation Army
INRI	*Iesus Nazarenus Rex Iudaeorum* = Jesus of Nazareth, King of the Jews
INSET	in-service education and training
Inst	institute
inst	instant; instrument
INTELSAT	International Telecommunications Satellite Organisation

Internet Abbrajargon

Inspired perhaps by the rich profusion of computer abbreviations and acronyms, the Internet is fast catching up with its own brand of abbrajargon. Some of the more vital Internet terms, such as HTML, URL, and ISP have their own entries in this book. The following examples are among the many, many 'chat' terms increasingly used on the web.

AFAIK	As far as I know
BBS	Bulletin Board System
BTW	By the way . . .
CYA	See ya
FAQ	Frequently asked questions
FWIW	For what it's worth . . .
FYEO	For your eyes only
G/S?	Are you gay or straight?
IMHO	In my humble opinion . . .
KIT	Keep in touch
RTFM	Read the f*****g manual
TIA	Thanks in advance
TVM	Thanks very much

Interpol	International Criminal Police Organisation
intl	internal; international
inv	*invenit* = designed by; *inv et del* = designed and drawn by (on antique prints and engravings)
INTUC	Indian National Trade Union Congress
IO	intelligence officer
IOC	International Olympic Committee
IOF	Independent Order of Foresters (friendly society)
IOM; IoM	Isle of Man
IOJ	International Organisation of Journalists
IOOF	Independent Order of Oddfellows (friendly society)
IOU	I owe you
IOW; IoW	Isle of Wight

IP	Internet protocol
IPA	International Phonetic Alphabet; Institute of Practitioners in Advertising; International Publishers' Association; India pale ale
IPAA	International Prisoners' Aid Association
IPARS	International Programmed Airline Reservation System
IPC	International Publishing Corporation
IPR	Institute of Public Relations
ips	inches per second
IPTPA	International Professional Tennis Players' Association
IPU	Inter-Parliamentary Union
IQ	intelligence quotient
iq	*idem quod* = the same as
IR	Inland Revenue; infrared
Ir; Ire	Ireland
IRA	Irish Republican Army
iran	inspect and repair as necessary
IRBM	intermediate-range ballistic missile
IRC	International Red Cross
IRF	International Rowing Federation
IRO	International Refugee/Relief Organisation; Inland Revenue Office; industrial relations officer
irreg	irregular
IRS	Internal Revenue Service (US)
ISA	individual savings account; **ISAS** = individual savings accounts
ISAM	Infants of Substance Abuse Mothers
ISBN	International Standard Book Number
ISC	Imperial Staff College; International Supreme Council (Freemasons)
ISD	international subscriber dialling
ISDN	Integrated Services Digital Network

ISF	International Shipping Federation
ISIS	Independent Schools Information Service
ISO	International Standards Organisation; Imperial Service Order
ISP	Internet Service Provider
ISPA	International Society for the Protection of Animals
ISS	Institute for Strategic Studies

Initials

Abbreviations are contractions, and therefore include initials, which are contractions of names: **GBS** for the dramatist George Bernard Shaw, or **NYC** for New York City. Other types of contractions are those of words, where all the middle letters are omitted (**Mr** for Mister); where the final letters are dropped (**cat** for catalogue); or where various bits of the word are dispensed with (**bldg** for building). An acronym results from creating initials to coincide with a recognised word, such as **CAUTION** (Citizens Against Unnecessary Tax Increases and Other Nonsense) or coining a new word, like **SNAFU** (situation normal, all fouled up).

ISSN	International Standard Serial Number
ISU	International Skating Union
IT	information technology
It, Ital	Italy; Italian
ITA	Initial Teaching Alphabet; Independent Television Authority (now the **IBA**); Institute of Travel Agents
ital	italic; italics
ITALY	I trust and love you
IT&T	International Telephone and Telegraph Corporation

ITC	Imperial Tobacco Company; Independent Television Commission
ITCA	Independent Television Contractors' Association
ITE	Institute of Terrestrial Ecology
ITGWF	International Textile and Garment Workers' Federation
ITMA	"It's that man again!"– title of 1940s radio show by comedian Tommy Handley
ITN	Independent Television News
ITO	International Trade Organisation
ITTF	International Table Tennis Federation
ITU	International Telecommunications Union; International Temperance Union; intensive therapy unit
ITV	independent television
ITWF	International Transport Workers' Federation
IU, iu	international unit
IUD	intra-uterine device (also **IUCD** = intra-uterine contraceptive device)
IUS	International Union of Students
IV	Roman numeral for four (4)
IVA	interim voluntary arrangement (bankruptcy proceedings)
IVB	invalidity benefit
IVBF	International Volley-Ball Federation
IVF	in vitro fertilization
IVR	International Vehicle Registration
IWTA	Inland Water Transport Association
IWW	Industrial Workers of the World
IYHF	International Youth Hostels Federation
IYRU	International Yacht Racing Union

J

Jeevesian Abbreviations

It seems appropriate that the comic author P G (for Pelham Grenville) Wodehouse should have been attracted to the abbreviation, and he created many of them for his most famous character, Jeeves:

see at a g	see at a glance	**hwb**	hot water bottle
break the n	break the news	**a hollow g**	a hollow groan
the inev	the inevitable	**fb**	fevered brow
nervous s	nervous strain	**the posish**	the position
eggs and b	eggs and bacon	**cut it s**	cut it short

J	jack (cards); joule (unit of electrical energy); Jacobean; January; Jesus; Jew; Jewish; Journal; Judaic; July; June; Jurassic; Judge (**JJ** = Judges); Justice
JA	Judge Advocate; joint account (also **J/A**); Justice Appeal
Ja	January (also **Jan**)
JAA	Jewish Athletic Association
JAC	Junior Association of Commerce (US)
JAG	Judge Advocate General
Jag	Jaguar (car make)

JAL	Japan Air Lines; jet approach and landing chart (aeronautics)
Jam	Jamaica
Jan	January
J&B	Justerini and Brooks (brand of Scotch whisky)
J&K	Jammu and Kashmir
JANET	joint academic network (computers)
JAP	J A Prestwich &Co, auto and motorcycle engine maker; Jewish American princess
Jap	Japan; Japanese
jap	japanned
jar	jargon
JAT	*Jugoslovenski Aero-Transport* = Yugoslav Airlines
JATCRU	joint traffic control radar unit
JATO	jet-assisted take-off
jav	javelin (athletics)
JAYCEE	Junior Chamber of Commerce (also **JC**)
JB	*Juris Baccalaureus* = Bachelor of Laws
jb, JB	junction box (electric circuits)
JBC	Japan Broadcasting Corporation
JBES	Jodrell Bank Experimental Station
JBS	John Birch Society (US)
JC	Jesus Christ; *Jewish Chronicle*; Jockey Club; Julius Caesar; Junior Chamber of Commerce (and member of same); junior college (US); juvenile court
J-C	*Jesus-Christ* = Jesus Christ (in French)
JCB	Initials of Joseph Cyril Bamford, inventor of the internationally used earth-moving machines; Bachelor of Canon Law
JCC	Jesus College, Cambridge; Junior Chamber of Commerce
JCI	Junior Chamber International
JCNAAF	Joint Canadian Navy-Army-Air Force
JCL	job control language (computers)

JCR	junior common room
JCS	Joint Chiefs of Staff; Joint Commonwealth Societies
jct	junction
JD	Justice Department (US); Diploma in Journalism; juvenile delinquent
jd	joined
JEC	Joint Economic Committee (US Congress)
Jer	Jersey; Jerusalem
JET	Joint European Torus (nuclear fusion research machine)
JEEP	Straying acronym meant to express General all-purpose Vehicle (**GP**). Thus Willy's GP became the famous Willy's Jeep
Jes Coll	Jesus College, Oxford
JETRO	Japan External Trade Organisation
JFK	John Fitzgerald Kennedy, former US president; New York airport
JHS	junior high school
JICNARS	Joint Industry Committee for National Readership Surveys
jnr	junior (also **jr**)
joc	jocular
JOGLE	John o'Groats to Land's End
journo	journalist
JP	Justice of the Peace
JUD	Doctor of Canon and Civil Law
jur	juror
JRC	Junior Red Cross
jt	joint
Jul	July
Jun	June
jurisp	jurisprudence
juv	juvenile

JW	Jehovah's Witness (religious organisation)
JWB	Jewish Welfare Board
jwlr	jeweller
JWT	J Walter Thompson advertising agency
JWU	Jewish War Veterans

Jokey Acronyms

Most of us know what **SNAFU** means, but how about **SUSFU** (Situation Unchanged; Still Fouled Up) and **REPULSE** (Russian Efforts to Publish Unsavoury Love Secrets of Edgar)? The latter acronym refers to an alleged Russian-backed campaign to discredit the former American FBI chief J Edgar Hoover. However its purpose was, you might say, **OTE** (Overtaken By Events) on Hoover's death in 1972. On the other hand, it might have been subject to **FUBB** (Fouled Up Beyond Belief).

K

K	kelvin (unit of thermodynamic temperature); Cretaceous (geology); Russian kopek; Papua New Guinea kina, Laotian kip, Zambian kwacha, Burmese kyat (currency units); king (chess, cards); Kirkpatrick (catalogue of Scarlatti's works); Köchel (catalogue of Mozart's works – qv **KV**); strikeout (baseball); one thousand
k	karat (also **kt**); killed; kilo; king (also **K**)
k&b	kitchen and bathroom
KANU	Kenya African National Union
Kar	Karachi
Kash	Kashmir
kayo	knockout (boxing); also **KO**
KB	King's Bench; Knight Bachelor; king's bishop (chess); *Koninkrijk Belgie* = Kingdom of Belguim; kilobyte (computers)
kb	kilobar (physics)
KBC	King's Bench Court
kbd	keyboard
KBD	King's Bench Division
KBE	Knight Commander of the Order of the British Empire
KBES	knowledge-based expert system (computers); also **KBS**

Kbhvn	*København* = Copenhagen
KBP	king's bishop's pawn (chess)
KBW	King's Bench Walk, London
kbyte	kilobyte
KC	King's Counsel; King's College; King's Cross, London; Knight Commander; Knights of Columbus; Kennel Club
kc	kilocycle
KCB	Knight Commander of the Most Honourable Order of the Bath
KCC	King's College, Cambridge
K cell	killer cell (immunology)
KCH	King's College Hospital, London
KCL	King's College, London
KCMG	Knight Commander of the Order of St Michael and St George
Kcs	Czechoslovakian koruna (currency unit)
kcs	kilocycles per second
KD	knocked down (at auction; also unassembled furniture, equipment etc); kiln dried; *Kongeriget Danmark* = Kingdom of Denmark; Kuwaiti dina (currency unit)
kd	killed
KDG	King's Dragoon Guards
KE	kinetic energy
Ken	Kensington, London; **S Ken** = South Kensington; Kenya
KEY	keep extending yourself
kg	kilogram (also **kilo**)
KG	Knight of the Most Noble Order of the Garter
KGB	*Komitet Gosudarstvennoye Bezopasnosti* = Russian State Security Committee police
KGCB	Knight of the Grand Cross of the Bath
KhZ, khz	kilohertz

KCB KNIGHT COMMANDER OF THE MOST HONOURABLE ORDER OF THE BATH
KGB RUSSIAN STATE SECURITY COMMITTEE POLICE
KBC KING'S BENCH COURT

kilo	kilogram (also **kg**)
KISS	keep it simple, stupid!
KKK	Ku Klux Klan, US anti-black organisation
KL	Kuala Lumpur, Malaysia
kl	kilolitre
KLM	*Koninklijke Luchtvaart Maatschappij* = Royal Dutch Air Lines
km	kilometre; **km/h** = kilometres per hour
kn	krona, krone; knot
Knt	Knight
KO	knockout (also **kayo**)
KofC	Knight of Columbus (also **KC**)
kop	kopek
kpr	keeper (cricket); **wkt kpr** = wicket keeper
Kr	krona; krone (also **Kn**)

K ration	Army emergency rations, WW2, the initial of its creator, American physiologist Ancel Keys
KRL	knowledge representation language (artificial intelligence)
KStJ	Knight of the Order of St John
Kt	Knight; karat
KV	*Kochel Verseichnis* = catalogue of Mozart's music by Ludwig von Kochel,1862; (also **K**). Thus **K.492** is Mozart's opera *Le nozze di Figaro (The Marriage of Figaro)*
kV	kilovolt
kW	kilowatt; **KWH** or **kWH** = kilowatt-hour
KWIC	key word in context
KWOC	key word out of context
KYD	keep your distance

Kt-KB3, B-KN5

A thrilling chess game lasting hours can be described in a couple of square inches of space, using internationally understood cryptic letters and numbers. To read chess moves you need to know the following abbreviations:

K	King	**Q**	Queen	**B**	Bishop
Kt	Knight	**R**	Rook	**P**	Pawn
–	moves to	**x**	takes	**Ch**	check!
ep	*en passant*	**O-O**	castles (**K**)	**O-O-O**	castles (**Q**)
...	move made by	**!**	good move	**?**	error

Pieces are further identified as belonging to the King or the Queen; thus **KKt** = King's Knight; **QR** = Queen's Rook, and so on. Pawns are identified by their position; thus **QBP** = Queen's Bishop's pawn which is set in front of a Queen's Bishop, and **KKtP** = King's Knight's pawn in front of a King's Knight.

L

L	Roman numeral for fifty (50); learner driver/rider; Liberal; lire; lira; lek; large; low; pound sterling (*libra* = **L** = **£**)
l	latitude; length; light; late; large; litre; left; low; lease/leasehold
LA	Legislative Assembly
Lab	Labour Party; Labour Party member/supporter; Labrador
lab	laboratory; label; labourer
LAC	leading aircraftman
LACW	leading aircraftwoman
LADDER	National Learning and Attention Deficit Disorders Association
LADIES	Life After Divorce Is Eventually Saner (activist group)
lag	lagoon
LAIA	Latin American Integration Association
LAM	London Academy of Music
lam	laminate
LAMDA	London Academy of Music and Dramatic Art
LAN	local area network
Lancs	Lancashire

LASER	light amplification by stimulated emission of radiation
Lat	Latin (also **L**); Latvia
lat	latitude
LATCC	London air traffic control centre
lav	lavatory
lb	pound weight (16 ounces avoirdupois)
LB	Bachelor of Letters
LBC	London Broadcasting Company
LBCH	London Bankers' Clearing House
lbd	little black dress
LBJ	Lyndon Baines Johnson, former US president
LBO	leveraged buyout
LBS	London Graduate School of Business Studies
LBV	late bottled vintage (port wine)
lbw	leg before wicket (cricket)
LC	Library of Congress
L/C	letter of credit
lc	lower case (typography); left centre (theatre); little change (weather)
LCC	Former London County Council
LCCI	London Chamber of Commerce and Industry
LCD, lcd	liquid crystal display; lowest common denominator
LCJ	Lord Chief Justice
LCM	London College of Music
lcm	lowest common multiple
L/Cpl	Lance Corporal
LD	Doctor of Letters; lethal dose
Ldg	Leading seaman
ldg	landing; leading; lodging
ldmk	landmark
Ldn	London (also **Lon**)
L-dopa	LevoDihydraOxyPhenylAlanine (used to treat Parkinson's disease)

LDP	Liberal-Democratic Party (also **Lib-Dem**)
ldr	leader; ledger
L-driver	learner driver
LDS	(Church of) Latter-day Saints
LE	labour exchange
LEA	Local Education Authority
LEB	London Electricity Board
LED	light-emitting diode
leg	legal; legation; legion; legislature; legitimate
Lego	*leg-godt* = play well (Danish)
Leics	Leicestershire
LEM	lunar excursion module
LEPRA	Leprosy Relief Association
LETS	local exchange trading system
LF	low frequency
LFB	London Fire Brigade
LGB	Local Government Board
lge	large (also **lg**); league
lgth	length
LGU	Ladies' Golf Union
LH, lh	left hand; **lhs** = left hand side; **LHD**, **lhd** = left hand drive
LI	Lincoln's Inn, London; Long Island (US)
Lib	Liberal; Liberal Party; Liberal Party member/supporter
lib	library; librarian; libretto
Lib Cong	Library of Congress, Washington (also **LC**)
Lib-Lab	Parliamentary alliance during 1920s
lic	licence; licensed; licentiate
Lieut	Lieutenant
LIFFE	London International Financial Futures Exchange
LIFO	last in, first out
LIHG	*Ligue Internationale de Hockey sur Glace* = International Ice Hockey Federation
LILO	last in, last out

lim	limit; limited
limo	limousine
lin	line; lineal; linear
Lincs	Lincolnshire
lino	linoleum
Lintas	Lever's international advertising service
liq	liquid; liquor
LISP	list processing (computer language)
lit	literally; literary; literature
litho	lithography
LittB	Bachelor of Letters/Literature
LittD	Doctor of Letters/Literature
LJ	Lord Justice
LL	London Library; Lord Lieutenant
LLB	Bachelor of Laws
LLD	Doctor of Laws
LLM	Master of Laws

Sorry... this train only goes as far as LLANFAIR. To get to the end of the sign, you have to catch another train...

NO SMOKING

LLANFAIR-PG   Llanfairpwllgwyngyllgogerych-wyrndrobwllllantysiliogogo-goch – a village in Anglesey, Wales

Llanfair-PG	Llanfairpwllgwyngyllgogerychwyrndrobwllllan-tysiliogogogoch, a village in Anglesey, Wales
lm	lumen (unit of light)
LMD	local medical doctor
LME	London Metal Exchange
LMH	Lady Margaret Hall, Oxford
LMR	Former London Midland Region of British Rail
LMS	Former London, Midland and Scottish Railway; local management of schools
LMus	Licentiate of Music
LNB	low noise block down converter (the gubbins mounted at the centre of a satellite dish)
LNER	Former London and North Eastern Railway
LNG	liquefied natural gas
Lnrk	Lanarkshire
LNWR	Former London and North Western Railway (also **L&NWR**)
LOA	leave of absence; Local Overseas Allowance (Civil Service)
loc	local; location; letter of credit
loco	locomotive
Lond	London
LOST	Law of the Sea Treaty
LOX, lox	liquid oxygen
LP	long playing (vinyl) record; Labour Party; life policy; Lord Provost; low pressure
L/P	letterpress (printing)
LPE	London Press Exchange
LPG	liquefied petroleum gas
L-plate	red-on-white L to indicate vehicle is driven or ridden by a learner-driver/rider
LPN	Licensed Practical Nurse
LPO	London Philharmonic Orchestra; local post office

Lewd Acronyms

Abbreviations are frequently used in the cause of euphemism. The socially acceptable word *pee* derives from the shortened '*p*' for the unacceptable *piss*. Other contractions include *WC* (water closet); *FA* (*sweet FA* = sweet fuck all, further euphemised to *sweet Fanny Adams*); *berk* (from the Cockney rhyming slang expression *Berkshire Hunt*); *sod* (short for *sodomite*) and *bumf* (*bum fodder*).

Then there are the so-called 'lovers' acronyms'. Several are listed in the main dictionary (**swalk**, **Holland**, **Burma**, etc) but here are some that are not: **EDINBURGH** (Elated, Darling, I'm Near. Book Usual Room Grand Hotel); **EGYPT** (Eager to Grab Your Pretty Tits) and **NORWICH** (kNickers Off, Ready When I Come Home). And of course there is the rare spotted unintentionally risque abbreviation of which this one, which appeared in the *Herald*, a Bedfordshire newspaper, is typical: "Sex crimes are on the increase in Beds".

L'pool	Liverpool
LPS	London Philharmonic Society; Lord Privy Seal
LRCA	London Retail Credit Association
Lrs	Lancers
LRSC	Licentiate of the Royal Society of Chemistry
LRT	London regional transport
LS	Law Society; Linnean Society; Licentiate in Surgery; long shot (film making); licensed surveyor
ls	signed letter; **als** = autograph signed letter
LSD	lysergic acid diethylamide (hallucinogenic drug); League of Safe Drivers; pounds, shillings and pence (£sd)
LSE	London School of Economics; London Stock Exchange
LS&GCM	Long Service and Good Conduct Medal
LSO	London Symphony Orchestra

LSSO	London Schools Symphony Orchestra
LST	local standard time
Lt	Lieutenant
LTA	Lawn Tennis Association
LTAA	Lawn Tennis Association of Australia
LTB	London Transport Board; London Tourist Board
Lt Cdr	Lieutenant Commander
Ltd, ltd	Limited (liability company) in the UK
Lt Gen	Lieutenant General
Lt Gov	Lieutenant Governor
ltr	litre
LU	loudness unit
lub	lubricate; lubricant; lubrication
lug	luggage
LV	luncheon voucher; licensed victualler
Lv	lev; leva
lv	low voltage; leave of absence
LVA	Licensed Victuallers' Association
LW	long wave (frequency); low water
LWB, lwb	long wheel base
LWL	length at waterline (shipping)
LWM	low water mark
LWONT	low water, ordinary neap tide
LWOST	low water, ordinary spring tide
LWT	London Weekend Television

M

Man Through The Ages

Most of us have become all too familiar with the Yuppie (Young UPwardly mobile Professional), coined in the early 1980s. Since then other acronymic age and social markers have surfaced, of which these are an amusing selection:

PUPPIE	Pregnant Urban Professional
YUMMIE	Young Upwardly Mobile Mother
DINKY	Double Income, No kids yet
BURPIES	Boozing Urban-Rural Parasites
OINK	One Income, No Kids
TRIUMPH	Two Rowdy Infants, Unemployed, Middleaged, Planning Hopefully
WOOPIE	Well Off Old Person
FAGEND	Five Adorable Grandchildren. Endlessly Needing Dosh
WOTCHA	Wonderful Old Thing, Considering His/Her Age
BIRO	Bedridden, Investments Running Out

M — *Monsieur*; Monday; Mach number; medium; million; mark; male; mile; medieval; Roman numeral for one thousand (1,000); Messier catalogue of nebulae and star clusters (1784);

the Secret Service chief in Ian Fleming's *James Bond* novels

m masculine; metre; member; meridian; mile; month; minute; mountain; maiden over (cricket scoring); *mille* (1,000); memorandum; middle

MAC mac

MACINTOSH COMPUTER STYLE OF RAINCOAT

MA	Master of Arts; Military Academy; mental age
MA&F	former Ministry of Agriculture and Fishing (*qv* **MAFF**)
ma'am	madam; madame
MAC	multiplexed analogue component
Mac	MacIntosh computer
mac	macintosh (style of raincoat); also mackintosh
Mach	Mach number (ratio between speed and speed of sound; Mach 1 is the speed of sound)
mach	machinery
MAD	mutual assured destruction; mean absolute deviation

MADD	Mothers Against Drunk Driving (US)
MAFF	Ministry of Agriculture, Fisheries and Food
mag	magazine; magnetic; magnitude
Magd	Magdalen College, Oxford
maitre d'	maitre d'hotel
Maj Gen	Major General
MAN	*Maschinen Augsburg-Nurnberg AG* (German firm)
M&B693	May and Baker 693, sulphapyridine, a pioneer sulpha drug
Man Dir	managing director (also **man dir, MD**)
m&b	mild and bitter (ale)
M&Ms	button-size chocolate-coated sweets
M&S	Marks and Spencer, department store chain
Man Ed	managing editor (also **man ed**)
MANWEB	Former Merseyside and North Wales Electricity Board
Mar	March
mar	married; marine; maritime
Marat/Sade	Short for *The Persecution and Assassination of Marat as Performed by the Inmates of Charenton under the Direction of the Marquis de Sade,* a play by Peter Weiss
marg	margarine (also **marge**)
Marq	Marquis
mart	market
MARV	manoeuvrable re-entry vehicle
masc	masculine (also **mas**)
MASH	Mobile Army Surgical Hospital (US); also the TV series
mat	matrix; matte; matinee; maternity; mature
maths	mathematics (**math** in the US)
Matric	Matriculation (higher education entry examination)
MAW	model, actress, whatever
max	maximum
MAYDAY	*m'aidez* = help me (distress call)

MB	Bachelor of Medicine; medical board; marketing board; maternity benefit; methyl bromide (fire retardant)
mb	millibar
MBA	Master of Business Administration (also "Mind my Bloody Arse" aimed at over-cautious young MBAs unable to make decisions)
MBE	Member of the Order of the British Empire
mbr	member
MC	Military Cross; master of ceremonies; Member of Congress (US)
mc	motorcycle (also **m/c**); megacycle
MCB	miniature circuit breaker
MCh	Master of Surgery
MCC	Marylebone Cricket Club; Melbourne Cricket Club
MCP	male chauvinist pig
MCPS	Mechanical Copyright Protection Society; Member of the College of Physicians and Surgeons
MCU	medium close-up (cinemaphotography)
MD	Doctor of Medicine; managing director; musical director; mentally deficient
MDA	Muscular Dystrophy Association
Mddx	Middlesex
MDF	medium-density fibreboard
MDR, mdr	minimum daily requirement
MDS	Master of Dental Surgery
mdse	merchandise
ME	marine/mechanical/mining engineer; Middle East; myalgic encephalomyelitis
mech	mechanical
MEd	Master of Education
Med	Mediterranean
med	medical; medicine; medium; median; medieval
MEF	Mediterranean Expeditionary Force

MEK	methyl-ethyl-ketone (industrial solvent)
Melb	Melbourne
mem	member; memorial; memorandum
Mencap	Royal Society for Mentally Handicapped Children and Adults
MEP	Member of the European Parliament
Mer	Merionethshire
mer	meridian
Merc	Mercedes (car)
MERLIN	Medium Energy Reactor, Light water Industrial Neutron source
Messrs	*Messieurs* = gentlemen
Met	Metropolitan Opera House, New York; meteorological office
met	metropolitan; meteorological
metall	metallurgy; metallurgical
Meth	Methodist
meths	methylated spirit (also **meth, metho**)
Metro	*Chemin de fer metropolitain* (Paris underground)
MeV	one million electron volts
Mex	Mexico; Mexican; **Tex-Mex** = Texan-Mexican food
MEZ	*Mitteleuropaische Zeit* = Central European Time
MF	medium frequency
MFB	Metropolitan Fire Brigade
MFD	minimum fatal dose
mfd	manufactured
mfg	manufacturing
mfr	manufacturer; manufacture
Mg	magnesium
MG	Morris Garage (sports cars)
mg	milligram; morning
MGB	*Ministerstvo gosudarstvennoye bezopasnosti* = former Soviet Ministry of State Security (renamed **KGB** in 1954)

MGM	Metro-Goldwyn-Mayer (Hollywood film studio)
MGN	Mirror Group Newspapers
mgr	manager
mgt	management
MHA	Member of the House of Assembly (Australia, Canada); Methodist Homes for the Aged
MHF	medium high frequency
MHR	Member of the House of Representatives (Australia, US)
MHW	mean high water
MHWNT	mean high water, neap tide
MHWST	mean high water, spring tide
MHz	megahertz
MIA	missing in action
MIAA	Member Architect of the Incorporated Association of Architects and Surveyors
MIBE	Member of the Institution of British Engineers
Mich	Michaelmas; Michigan
MICR	magnetic ink character recognition
MIDAS	missile defence alarm system
Middx	Middlesex (also **Mddx**)
MIF	milk in first (before pouring tea, coinsidcrcd non-U)
MI5	Section 5, Military Intelligence (British Government counter-intelligence agency)
MiG, MIG	Initials of Mikoyan and Gurevich, designers of Russian fighter aircraft of which the MiG-15 fighter, the supersonic MiG-19 and the MiG-21 fighter are the most notable
MIG	metal inert gas welding technique
mike	microphone
Mil	Military
mill	*millionen* = German million
MIMechE	Member of the Institution of Mechanical Engineers

MIMinE	Member of the Institute of Mining Engineers
MIMS	monthly index of medical specialties
MIMT	Member of the Institute of the Motor Trade
MIMunE	Member of the Institution of Municipal Engineers
Min	Minister; Ministry
min	minimum; mineralogy; minute; minor
MInstT	Member of the Institute of Technology
MIP	maximum investment plan; monthly investment plan
MIPS	million instructions per second (computers)
Miras	mortgage interest relief at source
MIRTE	Member of the Institute of Road Transport Engineers
MIRV	multiple independently targeted re-entry vehicle
misc	miscellaneous
MI6	Military Intelligence, Section 6 (British Government intelligence and espionage agency)
Miss	Mistress (originally, in 17th cent) – prefix for a girl or an unmarried woman
MIT	Massachusetts Institute of Technology
MITI	Ministry of International Trade and Industry (Japan)
MJQ	Modern Jazz Quartet
Mk, mk	mark (currency); mark (type of car)
mkt	market; **mktg** = marketing
ml	mililitre; mile
MLA	Member of the Legislative Assembly; Modern Language Association of America
MLC	Member of the Legislative Council (Australia, India)
MLD	minimum lethal dose
Mlle	*Mademoiselle* = Miss (in France)
MLR	minimum lending rate
MLS, mls	medium long shot (cinematography)
MLWNT	mean low water, neap tide

MLWST	mean low water, spring tide
MM	*Messieurs* = French equivalent of **Messrs** = plural of Mr; Military Medal; Mercantile Marine
mm	millimetre; mm^2 = square millimetre; mm^3 = cubic millimetre
MMDS	multipoint microwave distribution system (also **MDS**)
Mme, Mmes	*Madame* = Mrs; *Mesdames* = Ladies (in France)
MMQ	minimum manufacturing quantity
MMR	measles/mumps/rubella (combination childrens' vaccine)
MMus	Master of Music
MN	Merchant Navy
mng	managing; **Mng Dir** = managing director
mngr	manager (also **mgr**); **mngmt** = management
M-number	Number of nebulae and star clusters in Messier catalogue
MO	Medical Officer; Meteorological Office; mail order; money order

MO, M1, M2 . . . Money, Money, Money!

The prefix M followed by a numeral from 0 to 5 denotes the British Treasury's estimates of money supply – the amount of cash in circulation in actual notes and coins in your pockets and purses. The system works like this:

MO   Total amount of money in circulation added to all the banks' balances at the Bank of England

M1   Total amount of money in circulation, plus current and deposit accounts

M2   Total amount of money in circulation plus building society deposits, National Savings accounts and non-interest bearing bank deposits

M3	The total amount of **M1** plus total private-sector bank deposits and certificates of deposit
M3c	The total amount of **M3** plus foreign currency bank deposits
M4	The total amount of **M1** plus private sector bank deposits and holdings of money market instruments
M5	The total amount of **M4** plus building society deposits

Mo	Monday
mo	month; also used to indicate the size of a book's page, as in **12mo, 24mo, 32mo** and **64mo**, where a sheet is folded and cut to form 12, 24, 32 and 64 pages respectively; moment (as in *half a mo'*)
MOC	Mother of the Chapel (NUJ term)
MOD, MoD	Ministry of Defence
mod	moderate; modern
mod cons	modern coveniences
Model-T	Ford's first mass-produced car; 15 million produced between 1908 and 1927.
modem	modulator/demodulator; device for connecting a computer to a telephone
MOH	Medical Officer of Health
Moho	Mohorovicic discontinuity (the boundary between the earth's crust and mantle, after Croatian discoverer Andrija Mohorovicic)
MOMA	Museum of Modern Art, New York
Mon	Monmouthshire; Monday
M1, M2, B2065	Designation of British roads; **M** = motorway; **A** = Class 1 road; **B** = Class 2 road
Mons, M	*Monsieur* = Mr (in France)
Moped	motorised pedal cycle
MOPS	mail order protection scheme

MOR   middle of the road (radio music)

Mor	Morocco
mor	morocco (bookbinding)
MORI	Market and Opinion Research International (public poll)
MOS	metal oxide semiconductor; Mail on Sunday
mos	months
MOT	motor vehicle test certificate (Ministry of Transport)
Mounty	Royal Canadian Mounted Police (also **Mounties**)
MOUSE	Miniature Orbital Unmanned Satellite, Earth
MP	Member of Parliament; Military Police; Mercator's projection (cartography); Mounted Police
mp	melting point
MPA	Music Publishers' Association
mpc	maximum permissible concentration
MPG	main professional grade (teachers' salary scale)
mpg	miles per gallon
mph	miles per hour

MPLA-PT	*Movimento de Libertacao de Angola – Partido de Trabalho* = Popular Movement for the Liberation of Angola Workers' Party
MPO	military post office
MPS	Member of the Pharmaceutical/Philological/Physical Society
MPTA	Municipal Passenger Transport Association
MR	map reference; Master of the Rolls; motivational research
Mr	Mister; Master
MRA	Moral Rearmament
MRBM	medium range ballistic missile
MRC	Medical Research Council
MRE	meals ready to eat; meals rejected by Ethiopians (Br Army descr.)
MRH	Member of the Royal Household
MRI	magnetic resonance imaging
MRIA	Member of the Royal Irish Academy
MRP	manufacturer's recommended price
Mrs	Mistress (17th cent) prefix for a married woman
MRSC	Member of the Royal Society of Chemistry
MRT	mass rapid transport
MS	multiple sclerosis; medium shot (cinematography); Microsoft (computer software company); Master of Surgery; *memoriae sacrum* = sacred to the memory of (on gravestones)
Ms	Optional prefix for a woman, whether married or not
ms	manuscript (also **mss**)
m/s	metres per second
MSc	Master of Science
MS(Dent)	Master of Surgery (Dental Surgery)
MS-DOS	MicroSoft Disk Operating System (computers)
MSF	Manufacturing, Science, Finance (trade union)

MSG	monosodium glutamate (food flavour enhancer)
Msgr	Monsignor
MSI	medium scale integration
MSL	mean sea level
MST	Mountain Standard Time (N America)
mt	mount; mountain
MTB	motor torpedo boat
MTBE	methyl-tertiary-butyl ether (antiknock lead-free petrol additive)
MTech	Master of Technology
mtg	mortgage; meeting
MTV	Music Television (24-hour music channel)
MU	Musicians' Union; Manchester United Football Club; Mothers Union
mum	mother; chrysanthemum
mun	municipal
mus	museum; music; musical
MusB	Bachelor of Music
MusD	Doctor of Music
MV	market value; motor vessel; muzzle velocity
MVD	*Ministerstvo vnutrenhikh del* = former Soviet Ministry of Internal Affairs, succeeded by the KVD (Soviet Committee for Internal Affairs) in 1960
MVO	Member of the Royal Victorian Order; male voice over (TV and films)
MVS	Master of Veterinary Surgery
MVSc	Master of Veterinary Science
MW	Master of Wine; megawatt; medium wave
mW	milliwatt
MY	motor yacht
MYOB	mind your own business
mycol	mycology; mycological
myth	mythology; mythological
myxo	myxomatosis (Australia)

MI5, MI19 and the Secret World

MI5 is the section of the British Intelligence organisation responsible for internal security and counter-esponiage in Britain. **MI6** is the section responsible for international esponiage. The US has its **FBI** and **MI-8**, and the Republic of Ireland its **G2**. Spies love abbreviations!

Then, in Britain, there is **MI1** (Directorate of Military Intelligence); **MI3** (the former German section, Military Intelligence); **MI8** (Radio Security Service); **MI11** (Field Security Police) and **MI9** (Escape and Evasion Service). Not surprisingly each of these clandestine outfits spawns further shadowy initials: **D1** (Head of Russian counter-espionage); **SF** (phone tapping service); **GC&CS** (Government Code and Cipher School); **IIC** (Industrial Intelligence Centre) and the Butlins of the world of espionage, **WX**, a secret camp for spies on the Isle of Man.

N

N	North; Northern; Norway; Norwegian
n	name; near; negative; nephew; new; noon; north; northern; noun; number; neutral; neuter; normal
NA	North America
n/a	not applicable; not available
NAACP	National Association for the Advancement of Colored People
Naafa	North American Association for Fatness Acceptance
NAAFI	Navy, Army and Air Force Institutes (also **Naafi, Naffy**)
NAB	National Assistance Board; National Association of Broadcasters
NAC	National Advisory/Anglers'/Archives Council
NACF	National Art Collections Fund
NACRO	National Association for the Care and Resettlement of Offenders
nad	no appreciable difference; nothing abnormal detected
NAfr	North Africa
NAFTA	New Zealand and Australia Free Trade Agreement
NAGS	National Allotments and Gardens Society

NAHA	National Association of Health Authorities
NAI	nonaccidental injury
NAI register	national register of children considered to be at risk of abuse and injury from parents or guardians
NALGO	National and Local Government Officers' Association
NAMH	National Association for Mental Health
NAO	National Audit Office
NAPF	National Association of Pension Funds
NAPO	National Association of Property Owners
nar	narrow
NAS	Noise Abatement Society
NASA	National Aeronautics and Space Administration (US)
NASEN	National Association for Special Educational Needs
NAS/UWT	National Association of Schoolmasters/Union of Women Teachers
nat	native; natural; national; nationalist
NATCS	National Air Traffic Control Service
NATE	National Association for the Teaching of English
NATFHE	National Association of Teachers in Further and Higher Education
NATO	North Atlantic Treaty Organisation
NATSOPA	Former National Society of Operative Printers and Assistants
NATTKE	Former National Association of Theatrical, Television and Kine Employees
NatWest	National Westminster Bank
NAV	net asset value
nav	naval; navigable; navigation (also **navig**)
Nazi	*Nationalsozialisten* = German National Socialist Party member

NB, nb	*nota bene* = note well; no ball (cricket)
NBA	Net Book Agreement (former); National Boxing/ Basketball Association (US)
NBC	National Broadcasting Company (US)
NBG, nbg	no bloody good
NC	National Curriculum
nc, n/c	no charge
NCA	National Cricket Association
NCB	National Coal Board; no claim bonus
NCC	Nature Conservancy Council
NCCL	National Council for Civil Liberties
NCCVD	National Council for Combating Venereal Diseases
NCO	non-commissioned officer
NCP	National Country Party (Australia)
NCR	National Cash Register Company; no carbon/ copy required
NCU	National Cyclists' Union
NCVO	National Coucil for Voluntary Organisations
nd	no date (undated); not drawn; no decision
NDA	National Dairymens' Association
NDE	near-death experience
Ndl	Netherlands (also **Neth**)
NDP	net domestic product
NDT	non-destructive testing
nee	*nee* = French for born (ie, Mrs Joan Smith, nee Jones, indicates that Mrs Smith's maiden name was Jones)
NEA	North East Airlines (US)
NEB	National Enterprise Board; New English Bible
NEC	Nippon Electrical Company (Japan)
NEDC	National Economic Development Council (also **Neddy**, both now defunct)
ne'er	never
neg	negative

Neg	Negro
nem con	*nemine contradicente* = no contradictions; unanimous
NERC	Natural Environment Research Council
NESB	non-English speaking background (applied to some foreign immigrants in Australia)
NESTOR	NEutron Source Thermal reactOR
net	after all deductions (also **nett**)
Neth	Netherlands
neur	neurological
neut	neutral; neuter
NF	National Front
N/f, n/f	no funds
NFA	National Federation of Anglers
NFL	National Football League (US and Canada)
NFS	National Fire Service; not for sale
NFT	National Film Theatre, London
NFU	National Farmers' Union
NFUW	National Farmers' Union of Wales
NFWI	National Federation of Womens' Institutes
NFYFC	National Federation of Young Farmers' Clubs
NG	New Guinea; National Guard (US)
ng	no good; narrow gauge (railway)
NGA	National Graphical Association
NGC	New General Catalogue (of nebulae, galaxies and star clusters)
NGk	New Greek
NGL	natural gas liquids
NGO	non-governmental organisation
NGS	National Geographic Society
NHI	National Health Insurance
NHK	*Nippon Hoso Kyokai* = Japan Broadcasting Corporation
NHS	National Health Service
NI	National Insurance; Northern Ireland; News International

NIC	newly industrialised country; national insurance contribution
NICAM	near-instantaneous companding audio multiplex system (digital recording)
NIHE	National Institute for Higher Education
NII	nuclear installations inspectorate
NINA	no Irish need apply
Nimby	not in my backyard!
NIRC	National Industrial Relations Court
N Ire	Northern Ireland (also **N Ir**)
NIREX	Nuclear Industry Radioactive Waste Disposal Executive
NJ	nose job; New Jersey
NKr	krone (Norwegian currency unit)
NKGB	*Narodny komissariat gosudar stvennoye bezopasnosti* = People's Commissariat of State Security (1943-46)
NKVD	*Narodny komissariat vnutrennikh del* = People's Commissariat of Internal Affairs (Soviet police 1934-46)
NL	New Latin; no liability (Australia); Netherlands
NLF	National Liberation Front
NLS	National Library of Scotland
nlt	not less than; not later than (**nmt** = not more than)
NLW	National Library of Wales
nm	nanometre; nautical mile
NMGC	National Marriage Guidance Council
NMHA	National Mental Health Association
NMR	nuclear magnetic resonance scanner
NMU	National Maritime Union
NNP	net national product
no	number (**nos** = numbers); north; northern; not out (cricket)
No1	No 1, Apsley House, Piccadilly, London, former home of the Duke of Wellington

No10	No 10, Downing Street, London, the British Prime Minister's residence
nol pros	*nolle prosequi* = abandonment of court action by plaintiff in civil cases (also **nolle pros**)
nom	nomenclature; nominated; nominal
non res	non-resident
non seq	*non sequitur* = it does not follow, ie, a statement or conclusion that does not logically follow from what preceded
non-U	not upper class
NOP	National Opinion Poll
Nor	Norway; Norwegian
Norm	Norman
norm	normal
Northants	Northamptonshire
Northmb	Northumberland
NORWEB	Former North Western Electricity Board

An Initial Quiz

The answer to each of these questions is a single initial or letter from the first half of the alphabet. *Answers on page 116.*

1 Second most famous early Ford motor car (not the Model T)
2 Scrabble tile with a value shared by no other letter
3 First letter on the standard Snellen Eye Test chart
4 Highest key on an ordinary piano
5 A learner-driver must display it
6 James Bond's secret service chief

nos	numbers
Notts	Nottinghamshire
Nov	November

NoW	*News of the World* (Sunday newspaper)
NP	Notary Public; neuropsychiatry; noun phrase
np	new pence (Britain's decimal coinage introduced in 1971); new paragraph (printing); nickel plated
n/p	net proceeds (also **np**)
NPA	National Pigeon Association; Newspaper Publishers' Association
NPD	new product development
NPFA	National Playing Fields Association
NPK	nitrogen, phosphorus and potassium fertiliser
NPL	National Physical Laboratory
NPV	net present value; no par value
NQU	not quite us (social status observation)
nr	near
NRA	National Rifle Association
NRC	Nuclear Research Council
NRCA	National Retail Credit Association
NRF	National Relief Fund
NRFL	Northern Rugby Football League
NRS	National Readership Survey
NRV	net realisable value
NS	Nova Scotia; nuclear ship; not satisfactory
NSA	National Skating Association
NSAID	non-steroidal anti-inflammatory drug
NSB	National Savings Bank
NSC	National Safety Council
nsf	not sufficient funds (also **n/s, n/s/f**)
NSFGB	National Ski Federation of Great Britain
NSG	nonstatutory guidelines (education: National Curriculum)
NSPCC	National Society for the Prevention of Cruelty to Children
NSU	non-specific urethritis
NSW	New South Wales

NT	National Theatre, London; National Trust; Northern Territory (Australia); New Testament
Nth	North; Northern
NTP	normal temperature and pressure (meteorological)
NTS	National Trust for Scotland
NTSC	National Television System Committee (US body controlling colour television standards)
NTV	Nippon Television
nt wt	net weight
NUAAW	National Union of Agricultural and Allied Workers
NUJ	National Union of Journalists
num	numerical; numeral; number
numis	numismatics
NUM	National Union of Mineworkers
NUPE	National Union of Public Employees
NUR	National Union of Railwaymen
NURA	National Union of Ratepayers' Associations
NUS	National Union of Students/Seamen

Answers to Initial Quiz

1. The Ford Model A   2. The letter K   3. The letter F   4. High C
5. L for Learner   6. Mysteriously known as M

NUT	National Union of Teachers
NVQ	National Vocational Qualification
NWAWWASBE	Never wash a window with a soft boiled egg (slogan from the 1940s radio programme *It's That Man Again* (ITMA)
NY	New York
NYC	New York City
NYD	not yet diagnosed

NYO	National Youth Orchestra
NYPD	New York Police Department
NYSE	New York Stock Exchange
NYT	National Youth Theatre
NYTO	National Youth Jazz Orchestra
NZ	New Zealand
NZBC	New Zealand Broadcasting Commission
NZMA	New Zealand Medical Association
NZRFU	New Zealand Rugby Football Union
NZRN	New Zealand Registered Nurse

O

OAPs and Senior Citizens

For decades now there's been a constant search for a more dignified term to describe an old age pensioner (**OAP**) with its image of down-at-heel frailty. Drop the *P* and you have **OA**, or Older Adult, considered by some to be an improvement. The unfortunate **SS** for Senior Citizen was imported from the US in the 1940s (but didn't survive) and the **GA**s or Golden Agers arrived a couple of decades later. But now the chronologically challenged are having their lot redefined by a fresh rash of acronyms: **WOTCHA** (wonderful old thing, considering his/her age); **TEPID** (tastes expensive, pension inadequate, dammit!) and **HOPEFUL** (hard-up old person expecting full useful life.

O	ocean; human blood type, ABO group
o	octavo (paper size); old; owner; only; over (cricket)
O&E	operations and engineering
O&M	Ogilvie & Mather (advertising agency); organisation and method
OA	older adult
OAP	old age pensioner
OAPEC	Organisation of Arab Petroleum Exporting Countries
OAS	Organisation of American States; *Organisation de l'armee secrete* (former pro-French political organisation in Algeria)

OAU	Organisation of African Unity
OB	Old Bailey, London; outside broadcast; old bonded whisky; old boy
OBAFGKMRNS	Classification of stars by US astronomer Henry Draper according to temperature and luminosity (mnemonic: *Oh Be A Fine Girl, Kiss Me Right Now, Susan*)
OBE	Order of the British Empire; one button exposed (shielded warning that a man's fly is open); other bugger's efforts
obit	obituary
obj	object; objective
obl	oblique; oblong
OBM	Ordnance Bench Mark
obs	obsolete (also **obsol**); obscure; observer; obstetrics; obstetrician
OC	Officer Commanding
oc	ocean (also **o**); office copy; over the counter
o/c	overcharge; overcharged
o'c	*of the clock* = o'clock
occ	occupation; occupational; occasional; occurrence
OCD	obsessive compulsive disorder
OCR	optical character recognition/reader
OCS	Officer Candidate School
Oct	October
oct	octavo (printing)
OCUC	Oxford and Cambridge Universities' Club
OD	Officer of the Day; outside diameter; overdose (**OD'd** = overdosed)
O/D	overdrawn; overdraft; on demand
ODA	Overseas Development Administration of the Foreign and Commonwealth Office
ODESSA	Ocean Data Environmental Sciences Services Acquisition; Organisation to aid escape of Nazi SS members after WW2

ODETTE	Organisation for Data Exchange Through Tele-Transmission in Europe
ODM	Ministry of Overseas Development
ODP	overall development planning
OE	Old English (language)
oe	omissions excepted
OECD	Organisation for Economic Cooperation and Development
OED	Oxford English Dictionary
OEDIPUS	Oxford English Dictionary Interpretation, Proofing and Updating System
OEEC	Organisation for European Economic Cooperation
OEM	original equipment manufacturer (computers)
o'er	over
OF	Old French (language)
off	official (also **offic**); office; officer
OFFER	Office of Electricity Regulation
OFGAS	Office of Gas Supply
oflag	*offizierslager* = German POW camp for captured Allied officers
OFS	Orange Free State (South Africa)
oft	often
OFWAT	Office of Water Services
OFT	Office of Fair Trading
OFTEL	Office of Telecommunications
OG	Officer of the Guard; original gum (philately)
og	own goal (football)
OGM	ordinary general meeting
OGPU	*Obedinennoe Gosudarstvennoe politicheskoe upravlenie* = All-Union State Political Organisation (Soviet police), 1923-34, Political Organisation (1924-34)
oh	overhead (also **o/h**); on hand
ohc	overhead camshaft
OIT	*Organisation internationale du travail* = International Labour Organisation

ojt	on the job training
OK, ok	alright; everything in order (also **okay; okeh**)
Okie	Migrant worker in 1930s California (from Oklahoma)
OLC	Oak Leaf Cluster (US military award); online computer
Old Test	Old Testament
O-level	Ordinary level examinations; now **GCSE**
OM	Order of Merit; ordnance map
OMM	*Officier de l'Ordre du Merite Militaire* = French military decoration
OMS	*Organisation Mondiale de la Sante* = World Health Organisation
on appro	on approval
ONC	Ordinary National Certificate
OND	Ordinary National Diploma
ono	or nearest offer
Ont	Ontario, Canada
ont	ordinary neap tide
OOD	Officer of the Deck
OOG	Officer of the Guard
ooo	of obscure origin (dictionary term)
o/o/o	out of order
007	British Secret Service codename for Ian Fleming's fictional spy James Bond
OOW	Officer of the Watch
OP	out of print; old people; other person
op	operation (**ops** = operations); operator; operational; opposite (also **opp**); optical; opaque
Op art	optical art (optically influenced designs, launched in 1960s)
op cit	*opere citato* = in the work cited
OPC	ordinary Portland cement
OPEC	Organisation of Petroleum Exporting Countries

OPEX	operational, executive and administrative personnel
ophth	ophthalmic
opp	opposite (also **op**); opposed
opr	operator
opt	optical; optician; optimum; optional
OR	official receiver; orderly room; other ranks
or	owner's risk; overhaul and repair (also **o/r**)
ORBIS	orbiting radio beacon ionospheric satellite
ORBIT	on-line retrieval of bibliographical information
orch	orchestra
ord	ordained; ordinary; ordnance
org	organisation; organic; organ
orig	original; origination
O-ring	rubber oil seal ring used in machinery
orn	ornithology (also **ornith**); ornamental
Orth, orth	Orthodox (religion); orthopaedic; orthography
o/s, OS	out of stock; out of service; outsize; ordinary seaman; operating system (computers)
OSA	Order of Saint Augustine
OSB	Order of Saint Benedict
OSD	Order of Saint Dominic
o'seas	overseas
OSF	Order of Saint Francis
OSS	Office of Strategic Services (US)

Oz Abbros

Australians are loth to use long words and they are ferocious verbal surgeons. But they also possess the curious habit of adding an 'o' at the end of words they abbreviate:

arvo	afternoon	**garbo**	garbage collector
aspro	aspirin	**kero**	kerosene
commo	communist	**metho**	methylated spirit
doco	documentary	**preggo**	pregnant

AUSTRALIANS POSSESS THE CURIOUS HABIT OF
ADDING 'O' AT THE END OF WORDS THEY ABBREVIATE

OST	Office of Science and Technology
OT	overtime; occupational therapy; Old Testament (also **Old Test**)
OTB	off-track betting (US)
otc	over the counter
OTC	Officer Training Corps
OTE	on target earnings
OTL	overturned lorry
OTT	over the top
OU	Oxford University; Open University
OUP	Oxford University Press
ov	over; overture
OWLS	Oxford Word and Language Service
OXFAM, Oxfam	Oxford Committee for Famine Relief
Oxon	*Oxoniensis* = Oxford; Oxford University; Oxfordshire

Oxbridge   Oxford-Cambridge; also used to describe the older, classical universities in the UK

Oz   Australia
oz   ounce (**ozs** = ounces)

P

PORC : Protests, Organisations, Rallies and Causes

First, you find a cause. Then you organise a protest. And on the way you invent an acronym, usually by juggling the initials of your organisation to form a sympathetic nonce word or to fit an appropriate existing word. Create a good attention-getting acronym and you could win an award from **GOAL** (*Get Onomatopoetical Acronymic Lyricism*). Some of the the following, some from Britain but mostly from the US, present and past, must have been sure-fire winners:

CRASH: Citizens to Restrict Airline Smoking Hazards
MAMA: Mothers Against Murder and Aggression
SCRAM: Scottish Campaign to Resist the Atomic Menace
HOPE: Help Obese People Everywhere
POWER: Professionals Organised for Women's Equal Rights
APART: Absent Parents Asking for Reasonable Treatment
MOMS: Mothers for Moral Stability
POPS: Parents Opposed to Pornography in Schools
SCUM: Society for Cutting Up Men
WORMS: World Organisation to Restore Men's Supremacy
MEDIA: Move to End Deception In Advertising
GOO: Get Oil Out! (California protest against leaking drilling platforms)

LIFE:	Let's Improve Future Environment
CANDLES:	Children of Auschwitz, Nazi's Deadly Laboratory Experiments Survivors
TIP:	Turn In a Pusher (narcotics campaign)
WOMB:	Foundation for the Welfare of Mothers and Babies
CURSE:	Committee United to Revive Streaking Events

P	Post Office (on maps); park; parking; postage; pawn (chess); pedestrian; Protestant; public; port; positive
p	page; paragraph; passed (exams); penny; pence; peso; peseta; piastre; pint; post; population; present
PA	personal assistant; Patients' Association; personal allowance (tax); public address (system); press attache; prosecuting attorney; Publishers' Association; purchasing agent; press agent
pa	per annum
P/A	power of attorney; private account
PABX	private automatic branch exchange telephone system
PAC	Pacific Air Command (US)
Pac	Pacific
PACE	Police and Criminal Evidence Act; precision analogue computing equipment; performance and cost evaluation
pad	paddock
Page 3	Bare-breasted pinups featured on page 3 of *The Sun* newspaper
PAIS	partial androgen insensitivity syndrome; **AIS** = androgen insensitivity syndrome
PAL	phase alternation line (625-line British TV standard from 1967)
Pal	Palestine; palace

pal	palaeontology; palace
p&l, P&L	profit and loss
pamph	pamphlet
Pan	Panama
pan	panchromatic (photographic film)
Pan-Am	Pan-American Airways
P&G	Procter and Gamble (manufacturers)
panto	pantomime
P&O	Peninsular and Oriental (steamship company)
p&p	packing and postage
Pap-NG	Papua-New Guinea
Pap test	*Papanicolaou smear* = cervical smear test for precancerous cells named after its inventor George Papanicolaou
P&Q	peace and quiet: prison term for solitary confinement
PA	Press Association
par	paragraph; parallel; parish; parochial; parenthesis
para	airborne parachute troop (**paras** = plural)
Parl	Parliament; parliamentary
parl proc	parliamentary proceedings
part	participle; particular
PAs	Popular mountaineering boots, named after climber Pierre Allain
pass	passenger; passenger train
PA system	public address system
Pat, pat	Patent; patented (also **patd**); **pat pend** = patent pending
PATA	Pacific Area Travel Association
pathol	pathology; pathologist
Pat Off	Patent Office
PATSY	Performing Animal Top Star of the Year (Hollywood movie award)
PAU	Pan American Union

PAWC	Pan-African Workers' Congress
PAX	private automatic telephone exchange

Poms, Pommies and POMEs

The English and Australians will argue forever about the derivation of **Pom** and **Pommie**, the nicknames by which English people are known Down Under. A reddish or sunburned complexion, likened to a ripe apple, or worse, a pomegranate? Well, no. The most accepted etymology is a term supposedly used during the early nineteenth-century convict era when most immigrants in Australia were decidedly unwilling *Prisoners Of Mother England* or **POMEs**, later shortened to **POMS**.

PAYE	pay as you earn (income tax payment system)
PB	prayer book; personal best
PBI	poor bloody infantry
pbk	paperback (book)
PBM	permanent benchmark (surveying)
PBX	private branch telephone exchange
PC	Police Constable (also **Pc**); Privy Councillor; politically correct; personal computer; Progressive Conservative (Canada); parish council; parish councillor
pc	per cent; percentage; piece; postcard
P/C, p/c	petty cash; price current
PCB	printed circuit board
PCC	parochial church council
PCI	potential criminal informant
pcl	parcel
PCOS	polycystic ovary syndrome
PCP	phencyclidine, depressant drug (aka angel dust)
PCR	polymerase chain reaction (DNA reproduction)
PD	Police Department; production department

pd	paid; passed; postage due; post dated (also **p/d**)
PDA	public display of affection; personal digital assistant
pdq	pretty damn quick!
PDR	price-dividend ratio
PE	physical education; probable error
P/E	price-earnings ratio; port of embarkation; part-exchange
Pem	Pembrokeshire
PEN Club	International Association of Poets, Playwrights, Editors, Essayists and Novelists
Pen, pen	Peninsula; penitentiary
PEP	personal equity plan (tax advantage savings scheme); political and economic planning
PER	Professional Employment Register
per	*per procurationem* = on behalf of; every or each, eg, three serves per person; person; period
P/E ratio	price-earnings ratio
per cent	*per centum* = of every hundred (ie six per cent or 6% = six hundredths of the whole)
perf	perforated (philately); perfect; performance
perfin	perforated with initials (philately)
PERK	physical evidence recovery kit (forensics)
perk	perquisite
perm	permanent wave (hairstyle); permutation (pools)
perp	perpendicular
pers	person; personal
PERT	programme evaluation and review technique
PET scan	positron emission tomography
pet	petroleum; petrology
Peta	People for the Ethical Treatment of Animals
Pf, pf	pfennig (also **pfg**); perfect; preferred
Pfc	Private First-Class (US Army)
PFI	Public Finance Initiative
PFP	Passports For Pets. Changed from **FIDO** (qv) following complaints from cat lovers

PG PARENTAL GUIDANCE REQUIRED

PG	parental guidance required (motion picture classification); post graduate
pg	page
PGA	Professional Golfers' Association
PGR	parental guidance recommended (Australia) qv **PG**
pH	potential of hydrogen = measurement scale of acidity and alkalinity
ph	phase; philosophy (also **phil, philos**); phone
pharm	pharmaceutical; pharmacy; pharmacist
PHC	pharmaceutical chemist
PhD	Doctor of Philosophy (also **DPhil**)
Phil	Philharmonic; Philadelphia (also **Phila, Philly**); Philippines
phil	philology (also **philol**)
philos	philosophy; philosopher
phon	phonetic; phonetics; phonetically
phot	photography; photographic
phr	phrase
PHS	Printing House Square, London (former address of *The Times*)
phys	physician; physicist; physics; physical
physio	physiotherapy

physiol	physiological
physog	physiognomy
PI	per inquiry; petrol injection; programmed instruction, Philippine Islands
PIA	Personal Investment Authority

PIX, NIX and Varietyese

The US showbusiness journal *Variety* once published one of the world's greatest abbreviated headlines: **STIX NIX HIX PIX**, meaning that out-of-town and country moviegoers were not fans of films about rural America. If you can translate a headline like that you should have little trouble with **HANK CINQ** (when Sir Laurence Olivier's *Henry V* bombed in the US); nor with another classic: **HIP NIP IN HUB** (describing the visit of a Japanese jazzman to Boston, which is widely known as 'The Hub').

pic	picture; pictorial
PID	pelvic inflammation disease
PIE	Paedophile Information Exchange (banned organisation)
PIN	personal identification number
PinC	Priest in charge
pix	motion pictures
pixel	picture element (computers)
pk	park (also **P**); pack; peak
pkg	package
pkt	packet
PL	Plimsoll line (safe loading line on ships)
Pl	Place
pl	place; plain; plate; plural
P&L	profit and loss
PLA	Port of London Authority; People's Liberation Army (China)

plat	platoon; plateau; platform
PLATO	programmed logic for automated learning operation
PLC, plc	public limited company
PLN	Nationalist Party, Nicaragua
PLO	Palestine Liberation Organisation
PLP	Parliamentary Labour Party
PLR	Public Lending Right
plur	plural
Plum	Pelham = nickname for two celebrities: the comic author PG (Pelham Grenville) Wodehouse; and the English cricketer Sir Pelham Warner
PLUTO	pipeline under the ocean (supplied Allied forces during the Normandy landing in WW2)
Ply	Plymouth
PM	Prime Minister; Police Magistrate; Provost Marshal; postmaster; paymaster
pm, PM	*post meridiem* = after noon; post mortem
PMG	Postmaster General; Paymaster General
pmh	past medical history
pmk	postmark
PMS	premenstrual syndrome; Pantone matching system (colour printing)
PMT	premenstrual tension; photomechanical transfer (graphics)
pmt	payment
PN	promissory note (also **P/N; pn**)
PND	postnatal depression
PNdB	perceived noise decibel
PNG, png	*persona non grata* = unacceptable or inadmissible person
pntr	painter
PO	Post Office; postal order; Pilot Officer; Petty Officer; personnel officer; power operated

po	chamberpot
POB	post office box
POC	port of call
POD	pay on delivery
POE	port of entry/embarkation
POETs day	piss off early, tomorrow's Saturday (ie, it's Friday)
POL	petroleum, oil and lubricants
Pol	Poland; Polish
pol	police; political; politician; polarise
polio	poliomyelitis
poly	polytechnic (college)
POM	prescription-only medicine; qv article *Poms, Pommies and POMEs*
POP	post office preferred (envelope size); Point of Presence (Internet 'phone exchange')
Pop	*popina* = cookshop, Eton club that maintains school discipline
pop	population; point of purchase; popular (music)
Pop art	art with allusions to popular culture, launched in 1950s
por	portion; portrait (also **port**); porous
PORIS	Post Office Radio Interference Station
porn	pornography; pornographic
Port	Portugal; Portuguese
port	portable; portrait

Portmanteau Words

As they result from the blending of two or more words, portmanteau words are close relatives of acronyms. A selection:

agitprop	from AGITate and PROPaganda
avionics	from AVIation and electrONICS
brunch	from BReakfast and lUNCH
camcorder	from CAMera and reCORDER

chunnel	from CHannel and tUNNEL
cyborg	from CYBernetics and ORGanism
denim	from serge DE NIMes (in France, where it was developed)
moped	from MOtorbike and PEDal
motel	from MOTorcar and hotEL
napalm	from NAPhthalene and pALMitate
prissy	from PRIm and siSSY
simulcast	from SIMULtaneous and broadCAST
sitcom	from SITuation and COMedy
smog	from SMoke and fOG
squiggle	from SQUirm and wrIGGLE
Swatch	from SWiss and wATCH
Velcro	from VELour and CROche (French for 'hooked')

---

pos	position (also **posn**); point of sale; positive
POSSLQ	person of opposite sex sharing living quarters
poss	possible; possibility; possession
posse	*posse comitatus* = assembly of able-bodied men called by a town's sheriff to help maintain law and order
POST	point of sale terminal
posthum	posthumous
pot	potential
POUNC	Post Office Users' National Council
POV	point of view (cinematography); privately owned vehicle; peak of operating voltage
POW	prisoner of war
PP	parliamentary papers; parish priest; past president; parcel post
pp	pages; *per procurationem* = by proxy or by delegation to; post paid; pre-paid; parcel post; privately printed

PPA	Periodical Publishers' Association; Pools Proprietors' Association
pp	post paid; pre-paid (also **pp**)
PPE	philosophy, politics and economics (university course)
PPL	private pilot's licence
ppm	parts per million
PPP	personal pension plan; Penelope's pony paddock (used by estate agents to describe a small field attached to a country cottage); Private Patient's Plan; purchasing power parity (banking)
PPS	Parliamentary Private Secretary
pps	*post postscriptum* = an additional postscript
PQ	parliamentary question; Parti Quebecois (Canada)
pq	previous question
PR	proportional representation; public relations; postal regulations; progress report; Puerto Rico
pr	pair (**prs** = plural); per; present; print; printer; painter; price
pram	perambulator (baby carriage)
PRB	Pre-Raphaelite Brotherhood (19thC artists' group)
PRC	People's Republic of China
preb	prebendary
pref	preface; preferable; prefect; preference; preferred; preferential
prefs	preference shares; preferred stock
prefab	prefabricated
prelim	preliminary (**prelims** = introductory pages of a book)
prem	premium; premature infant
premed	premedical (usually preparing patient for an operation)
prep	preparatory; **prep school** = preparatory school
Pres	President; Presbyterian (also **Presb**)

pres	present
prev	previous; previously
pri	private (also **pvt, priv**); priority
prim	primary; primitive; primate
Prin	Principal; Principality
prin	principal; principle
PRO	public relations officer; Public Records Office
pro	professional
pro-am	professional-amateur (sport)
prob	probable; problem; probate
proc	proceedings (eg **Proc Roy Soc** = *Proceedings of the Royal Society*); process
prod	product; production; producer; (In Northern Ireland) Protestant
Prof	Professor
prog	programme; prognosis; progressive
prole	proletarian
PROLOG	programming logic, a mathematical logic-based computer language
PROM	programmable read-only memory (computers)
promo	promotion
Proms	Annual Albert Hall Promenade Concerts in which certain sections of the audience can walk about (or promenade) during performances
pron	pronounced; pronunciation; pronoun
prop	property (**props** = theatrical property); proposition; propeller; proprietor (also **propr**); proprietary; proper
Prot	Protestant; Protectorate
pro tem	*pro tempore* = for the time being
prov	province; provincial; provisional; proverb
Provo	Provisional = member of the Provisional Irish Republican Army
PRS	Performing Right Society Ltd

Mind your Ps and Qs

There are various derivations for this peculiar catchphrase, meaning, 'Look sharp, be careful, mind your manners, and behave properly'. One has it that *'p's and q's'* meant pints and quarts, probably of ale; the admonition warning either against over-indulgence, or of being overcharged. Another explanation is that printers, in the days of setting type by hand, had to watch their *p's* and *q's* as they looked much the same. And still another – perhaps the derivation most widely accepted – is that the term is simply an abbreviation of *please* and *thank-yous*.

PRT	petroleum revenue tax
Pru	Prudential Assurance Company Ltd
PS	Police Sergeant; Philological Society; public school; private secretary: Parliamentary Secretary
ps, PS	*post scriptum* = postscript
PSA	Property Services Agency; Public Service Association (New Zealand); pleasant Sunday afternoon; prostate specific antigen
PSAB	Public Schools Appointments Bureau
PSB	Premium Savings Bond
PSBR	public sector borrowing requirement
pseud	pseudonym; a pretentious person (also **pseudo**)
psf	pounds (lbs) per square foot
psi	pounds (lbs) per square inch
PSI	Policy Studies Institute
PSK	phase shift keying (digital data modulation system)
PSL	private sector liquidity
PST	Pacific Standard Time (N America)
PSTN	public switched telephone network
PSV	public service vehicle
PT	Public Trustee; pupil teacher; physical training
Pt	Port; Point

pt	part; pit; point; past tense; patient
PTA	Parent-Teacher Association; Passenger Transport Authority
pta	peseta
PT boat	patrol torpedo boat
ptd	printed; painted
PTE	Passenger Transport Executive
ptg	printing
PTI	physical training instructor
PTO	please turn over; power take-off
pt/pt	point to point (horse racing)
PTS	Philatelic Traders' Society
pts	parts; payments; pints; points
Pty	proprietary = private limited company (Australia, NZ, S Africa)
pub	public house; published (also **publ**); publisher; **pub date** = date on which a book is to be published
pud	pudding; pick up and deliver
pug	pugilist
punc	punctuation (also **punct**)
pur	purchase; purchased; purple; purify
PVA	polyvinyl acetate (plastic)
PVC	polyvinyl chloride (plastic)
PVR	premature voluntary retirement
PVS	Post-Vietnam syndrome
pvte	private
PWA	Public Works Administration (US); people with aids
PWD	Public Works Department
PWR	pressurised water reactor
PX	physical examination; US version of NAAFI
pxt	*pinxit* = he/she painted it (also **pinx, pnxt**)
PYO	pick your own

Some Curious Qs

If you convince others that **Qantas** is a word and not an acronym, you might also convince them that it is the only Q-word or name where the *'Q'* is not followed by the customary *'u'*. But is it? The *Chambers' Official Scrabble Words* lists 14, from *qadi* to *qintars*, none of which is ever likely to show up in the average person's vocabulary, plus of course *qwerty* which defines the standard typewriter or word-processor keyboard. On the other hand there are at least a score of abbreviations where the *'Q'* lacks its usual partner.

Q	Queen (royalty; chess; cards); Quebec (also **Que**); Queensland (also **Qld**); quartermaster (also **QM**); quetzal; quality
q	quarter; quarterly; quart; quarto; question; query; quire; quantity; quintal
Q&A	question and answer
QANTAS, Qantas	Queensland and Northern Territory Aerial Service (now the Australian international airline)
QB	Queen's Bench; **QBD** = Queen's Bench Division (law)
Qbc	Quebec
QC	Queen's Counsel; Queen's College

qe	*quod est* = which is
QE2	Queen Elizabeth II, Cunard Line cruise ship
QED	*quod erat demonstrandum* = which was to be proved
QF	quality factor
Q fever	query fever (from its unknown cause until late 1930s when it was discovered to be a viral infection)
QGM	Queen's Gallantry Medal
QHP	Queen's Honorary Physician
QHS	Queen's Honorary Surgeon
Qld	Queensland (also **Q**)
QM	Quartermaster; **QMG** = Quartermaster General
qnty	quantity
QPM	Queen's Police Medal
QPR	Queens Park Rangers Football Club
qq	quartos; questions
qqv	*quae vide* = which see (refers to more than one cross-reference); qv **qv**
qr	quarter; quarterly; quire (measure of paper and newspaper bundles
QS	quarantine station; quantity surveyor; Quarter Sessions (law)
QSGs	quasi-stellar galaxies
Q-ship	Armed merchant ship used as decoys (WW1) Also **Q-boat**
QSM	Queen's Service Medal (New Zealand)
QSO	Queen's Service Order (New Zealand)
Q-sort	'agree/disagree' psychological test
qt	quart (**qts** = quarts); quiet (**on the qt** = clandestinely)
qty	quantity
qu	question; query
quad	quadrangle; quadrant; quadruple
quake	earthquake

qual	qualification; quality
quango	quasi-autonomous non-governmental organisation
Que	Quebec (also **Q, Qbc**)
quot	quotation
qv	*quod vide* = which see (cross-reference to related item)
qu	query

A Question of being POSH

Professional etymologists have fairly effectively quashed the popular belief that the word *posh* – meaning upper-class, rich and fashionable – derives from *'port outward, starboard home'*. The phrase refers to the position of cabins on passenger ships that plied between Britain, India and the Far East during the Empire period; those away from the tropical sun being cooler and more desirable and thus only affordable by the toffs. The academic view is that *posh* was an old slang word for a dandy which fell out of use before returning to circulation in the late19th century. However the philological argument simmers on and romance, apparently, rather than logic, continues to persuade most of us that the popular belief is the true explanation.

R	rabbi; rand; railway; Reaumur (degree of heat); Republic; Republican; rector; registered (postal); river; Registered at the US Patent Office; Regiment; rupee; rook (chess); restricted (Australian film classification); rouble; route
r	radius; rare; right; red; road; rod; retired; railway; runs (cricket and baseball); rain; recipe; rouble
RA	Royal Academy; Royal Academician; Ratepayers' Association; Referees' Association; Royal Artillery; Ramblers' Association; Rear Admiral
RAA	Royal Academy of Arts
RAAF	Royal Australian Air Force
Rab	R A Butler, British Conservative politician
RAC	Royal Automobile Club; Royal Aero Club; Royal Agricultural College, Cirencester
RACE	rapid automatic checkout equipment
racon	radar beacon
Rad	Radnorshire
rad	radius, radian; radar; radio; radiology; radical; unit of radiation absorbed dose
RADA	Royal Academy of Dramatic Art
radar	radio detection and ranging
RADAS	random access discrete address system

R Adm	Rear Admiral
RAE	Royal Academy of Engineering; Royal Aircraft Establishment
RAEC	Royal Army Education Corps
RAF	Royal Air Force
RAFVR	Royal Air Force Volunteer Reserve
RAH	Royal Albert Hall, London
RAHS	Royal Australian Historical Society
RAI	*Radio Audisioni Italiane* = Italian Broadcasting Corporation
RAM	random access memory (computers); Royal Academy of Music
RAMAC	random access memory accounting (computers)
RAMC	Royal Army Medical Corps
RAN	Royal Australian Navy
R&A	Royal and Ancient Golf Club, St Andrews, Scotland
R&B	rhythm and blues (music)
R&CC	riot and civil commotions
R&D	research and development
r&r	rest and recreation; rock and roll
Ranji	K S Ranjitsinhji, Maharajah of Nawanagar, cricketer
RAOC	Royal Army Ordnance Corps
RATO	rocket-assisted takeoff
RAVC	Royal Army Veterinary Corps
RBA	Royal Society of British Artists
RBE	relative biological effectiveness
rbl	rouble (also **R, r**)
RBS	Royal Society of British Sculptors
RC	Red Cross; Roman Catholic; Reformed Church; Reserve Corps
rc	reinforced concrete
RCA	Royal College of Art; Royal Canadian Academy;

	Radio Corporation of America
RCAF	Royal Canadian Air Force
RCD	residual circuit device
rcd	received
RCM	Royal College of Music
RCMP	Royal Canadian Mounted Police
RCN	Royal College of Nursing; Royal Canadian Navy
RCO	Royal College of Organists
RCP	Royal College of Physicians
RCS	Royal College of Surgeons; Royal College of Science; Royal Corps of Signals

don't worry little girl – I'm a member of the RCS

YOU CRUEL, CRUEL MAN!

RCS   ROYAL COLLEGE of SURGEONS
RABBIT CLEARANCE SOCIETIES

RCSB	Royal Commonwealth Society for the Blind
RCT	Royal Corps of Transport
RCVS	Royal College of Veterinary Surgeons
rd, RD	road; rendered; round; rod; refer to drawer (also **RD, R/D**)

RDA	recommended daily allowance
RDC	Rural District Council
RDS	radio data system (transmission of digital signals)
RDT&E	research, development, test and evaluation
RDZ	radiation danger zone
RE	religious education; Royal Engineers; Reformed Episcopal
Re	rupee (also **Rs, rs** = rupees)
rec	received; receipt; recent; record; recorded; recreation; recipe
recce	reconnaissance
recd	received (also rec)
Rect	Rector; Rectory
rect	rectangular; rectify
red	reduced
ref	referee; refer; reference; refund (also **refd**)
Ref Ch	Reformed Church
Reg	Regina; Regent; registered (also **regd**)
reg	registered; regular; regulation; regiment

European Car Registration Letters

The letters GB, IRL, F and NL on motor vehicles are commonly seen and most of us know that they identify the country of registration: Great Britain, Ireland, France and the Netherlands (Holland). But what of GBJ or SLO? Here's an identification list of European motor vehicle code letters now increasingly seen on British roads:

A	Austria	**AL**	Albania	**AND**	Andorra	**B**	Belgium
BG	Bulgaria	**CH**	Switzerland	**CY**	Cyprus	**CZ**	Czech Rep
D	Germany	**DK**	Denmark	**E**	Spain	**F**	France
FL	Liechtenstein	**FR**	Faroe Is	**GB**	Britain	**GBA**	Alderney
GBG	Guernsey	**GBJ**	Jersey	**GBM**	Isle of Man	**GBZ**	Gibraltar

GR	Greece	**H**	Hungary	**I**	Italy	**IRL**	Ireland
IS	Iceland	**L**	Luxembourg	**M**	Malta	**MC**	Monaco
N	Norway	**NL**	Holland	**P**	Portugal	**PL**	Poland
RO	Romania	**RSM**	San Marino	**S**	Sweden	**SF**	Finland
SK	Slovak Rep	**SLO**	Slovenia	**V**	Vatican	**YU**	Yugoslavia

REGAL	range and elevation guidance for approach and landing (airports)
Reg Prof	Regius Professor
Reg TM	Registered Trade Mark (also **RTM**)
RI8 cert	British film classification (no under 18s admitted)
rej	reject
rel	relative; religion; relic; release
REM	rapid eye movement; Roentgen Equivalent in Man = unit measuring radiation exposure
REME	Royal Electrical and Mechanical Engineers
Renf	Renfrewshire
Rep	Republican (US)
rep	representative; repeat; repertory; reprint; repaired; report
repl	replace; replacement
repo	repossess; **repo man** = person hired to repossess goods
repr	represented; representative; reprint; reprinted
repro	reproduction
rept	receipt; report
req	request; requisition; required
res	residence; resident; reserved; reservoir; research; reservation; resolution; resigned
resig	resignation
resp	respectively; respondent
rest	restaurant (also **restr**)
ret, retd	retired; return; returned; retained

retro	retrorocket
Rev, Revd	Reverend
rev	reverse; revolution (**revs** = revolutions); revised; revision; review; revenue
Rev Ver	Revised Version of the Bible
rew	reward
RF	radio frequency; Royal Fusiliers; rugby football
RFC	Royal Flying Corps; Rugby Football Club
RFL	Rugby Football League
RFS	render, float and set (plastering)
RFSU	Rugby Football Schools' Union
RFU	Rugby Football Union
rgd	registered
RGN	Registered General Nurse
RGS	Royal Geographical Society
Rgt	Regiment
RH	Royal Highness; relative humidity; right hand
Rh factor	rhesus factor, inherited agglutinating agent in blood, first observed in rhesus monkeys
rh	right hand
RHA	Regional Health Authority; Royal Horse Artillery
rhd, RHD	right hand drive
rheo	rheostat
rhet	rhetorical
RHG	Royal Horse Guards
rhino	rhinoceros
R Hist S	Royal Historical Society
rhp	rated horsepower
RHS	Royal Historical Society; Royal Horticultural Society; Royal Humane Society
RI	Royal Institution, London; Royal Institute of Painters in Watercolours; *Regina et Imperatrix* = Queen and Empress; religious instruction
RIA	Royal Irish Academy

RIAA curve	international standard for microgroove disc reproduction
RIAC	Royal Irish Automobile Club
RIAI	Royal Institute of Architects in Ireland
RIAM	Royal Irish Academy of Music
RIBA	Royal Institute of British Architects
RIC	Royal Institute of Chemistry
RICS	Royal Institution of Chartered Surveyors
RIF	reduction in force (US euphemism for retrenchment)
RIIA	Royal Institute of International Affairs
RIP	*requiescat in pace* = rest in peace
RIS	Radio Interference Service
riv	river
RKO	Radio Corporation of America/Keith Orpheum Theatres; from 1931-53 one of the big Hollywood studios
RL	Rugby League
RLF	Royal Literary Fund
RLPAS	Royal London Prisoners' Aid Society
RLPO	Royal Liverpool Philharmonic Orchestra
RLS	Robert Louis Stevenson, writer and poet
RLSS	Royal Life Saving Society
rly	railway (also **rlwy**); relay
RM	Royal Marines; Royal Mail; registered midwife
rm	room; **rms** = rooms
RMA	Royal Military Academy, Sandhurst
RMC	Royal Military College
R-methodology	Statistically based psychological test (qv **Q-sort**)
rmm	relative molecular mass
R months	The eight months with 'r' in their names during which it is claimed that oysters may safely be eaten
RN	Royal Navy

RNA	ribonucleic acid
RNAS	Royal Naval Air Service; renamed Naval Air Command
RNC	Royal Naval College
RNIB	Royal National Institute for the Blind
RNID	Royal National Institute for the Deaf
RNLI	Royal National Lifeboat Institution
RNR	Royal Naval Reserve
RNVR	Royal Naval Volunteer Reserve
RNZAF	Royal New Zealand Air Force
RNZN	Royal New Zealand Navy
ro	run out (cricket); rowed over (rowing); run on (editing mark)
ROAM	return on assets managed
ROARE	reduction of attitudes and repressed emotions (sex offenders' treatment programme)
ROC	Royal Observer Corps
ROI	Royal Institute of Oil Painters; return on investment
Rolls	Rolls-Royce cars and engines
ROM	read-only memory (computers)
Rom	Roman; Romania; Romanian; Romance (languages)
roo	kangaroo
R101	British airship which crashed in 1930
rop	run of paper (newspaper publishing)
RORC	Royal Ocean Racing Club
RORC rating	Waterline length, sail area, beam and draught formula used to handicap racing yachts
RORO, roro	roll on/roll off (car and truck ferries)
ROSPA	Royal Society for the Prevention of Accidents
rot	rotary
Route 66	2,200 mile US highway running from Chicago to Los Angeles
ROW, row	right of way

Roy, roy	Royal; royalty
RP	received pronunciation; Royal Society of Portrait Painters; reply paid
Rp	rupiah
RPE	rate of perceived exertion (aerobics)
RPG	report programme generator (business computer programming language)
rph	revolutions per hour
RPI	retail price index
rpm	revolutions per minute; retail price maintenance (also **RPM**); reliability performance measure
RPO	Royal Philharmonic Orchestra; railway post office
RPS	Royal Photographic Society
rps	revolutions per second
rpt	repeat; reprint; report
RPV	remotely piloted vehicle
RQ	respiratory quotient
RR	railroad (US); Rolls-Royce; Right Reverend
RRB	Race Relations Board
RRP, rrp	recommended retail price
RS	Royal Society
Rs	rupees
RSA	Royal Scottish Academy/Academician; Royal Society of Arts; Returned Services Association (NZ); Republic of South Africa
RSC	Royal Shakespeare Company; Royal Chemical Society
RSE	Royal Society of Edinburgh
RSG	Regional Seat of Government; rate support grant
RSGB	Radio Society of Great Britain
RSI	Royal Sanitary Institute
RSJ, rsj	rolled steel joint
RSL	Royal Society of Literature; Returned Services League (Australia)

RSM	regimental sergeant major; Royal Society of Medicine; Royal School of Mines; Royal School of Music; Royal Society of Musicians
RSNC	Royal Society for Nature Conservation
RSNO	Royal Scottish National Orchestra
RSNZ	Royal Society of New Zealand
RSPB	Royal Society for the Protection of Birds
RSPCA	Royal Society for the Prevention of Cruelty to Animals
RSSPCC	Royal Scottish Society for the Prevention of Cruelty to Children
RSV	Revised Standard Version of the Bible
RSVP	*Repondez s'il vous plait* = reply if you please

RSVP REPONDEZ S'IL VOUS PLAIT
(REPLY IF YOU PLEASE)

RSWS	Royal Scottish Watercolour Society
rt	right
RTA	road traffic accident
RTB	return to base

rtd	returned; retired; **rtd ht** = retired hurt (cricket)
RTDS	real time data system
RTE	*Radio Telefis Eireann* = Irish Radio and Television
rte	route

The Three Rs

These, traditionally, are **readin', 'ritin' and 'rithmetic**. The phrase supposedly originated during the early years of the 19th century, when during a banquet, Sir William Curtis, an illiterate Lord Mayor of London, proposed a toast to education, or, as he put it, "readin, ritin and rithmetic".

RTF	Rich Text Format
rtg	rating
Rt Hon	Right Honourable
RTL	resistor transistor logic (electronic circuits)
RTM	registered trade mark
rtn	retain; return
RTR	Royal Tank Regiment
Rt Rev	Right Reverend
RTT	radioteletype
rtw	ready to wear
RTZ	Rio Tinto Zinc Corporation
RU	Rugby Union; Readers' Union
RUA	Royal Ulster Academy of Painting, Sculpture and Architecture
RUC	Royal Ulster Constabulary
RUG	restricted users group (computers)
RUI	Royal University of Ireland
RUKBA	Royal United Kingdom Beneficent Association
RUPP	road used as public path
RUR	*Rossum's Universal Robots*, Karel Capek's 1921 stage play

Rus	Russia; Russian (also **Russ**)
RV	Revised Version of the Bible; rateable value; research vessel; recreational vehicle; *Ryom Vivaldi Verzeichnis* = inventory of Vivaldi's compositions by Peter Ryom
RVCI	Royal Veterinary College of Ireland
rwd	rear wheel drive
RVO	Royal Victorian Order
RWS	Royal Society of Painters in Water Colour
Rwy	railway
RYA	Royal Yachting Association
RYS	Royal Yacht Squadron

S

Spoof Acronyms

It can be difficult separating real from spoof acronyms.
The Idaho Department of Law Enforcement found itself saddled with
an embarrassing acronym (**IDLE**), as did Coors Brewery in Colorado
when it set up an employee programme called Volunteers In
Community Enrichment (**VICE**). And IBM had a narrow escape
when it discovered that the acronym for its Forward Error Control
Electronics System was **FECES** (American for 'faeces'). It was quickly
renamed Data Correction System (**DACOR**). But not so lucky was
Buckinghamshire County Council when it renamed its Property
Service Group (a perfectly harmless **PSG**) Property Information and
Surveying Services (**PISS**). These, like the US Secretary of Defense
(**SOD**) and the US Pentagon's Missiles High-Speed Assembly Program
(**MISHAP**) are or were genuine acronyms. That's why the spoofs are
difficult to spot. It's only when you link the capitals of the Sam Houston
Institute of Technology in Texas that you realise that you've been had.
The British book trade journal *The Bookseller* fooled both its staff and
readers with a series of convincing French organisations: *Syndicat des
librairies universitaires et techniques* (**SLUT**); *Librairies universitaires de
syndicat techniques* (**LUST**) and the even more surreptitious *Federation
academique de redaction techniques* . . . .

S	Saint; Scotland; September; Senate; schilling; South; southern; Socialist; school; summer; *Senor; Signor; Signora;* sucre; Svedburg unit; sea; Sweden; Sabbath
s	section; sign; signed; southern; small; shilling; single; slow; spherical; stratus (cloud); sunny; *sur* = on (French place-names)
SA	South Africa; South Australia; *Societe Anonyme* (French/Belgium/Switzerland/Luxembourg limited liability company); *Sociedad Anonima* (Spanish and Portuguese limited liability company); South America; Society of Antiquaries/Arts/Authors; Salvation Army; *Sturmabteilung* = storm troopers; surface-to-air missile
sa	semi-annual; sex appeal
S/A	subject to approval/acceptance
SAA	South Africal Airways; small arms ammunition
SAAA	Scottish Amateur Athletic Association
SAAB	*Svensk Aeroplan Aktiebolag* (Swedish car, aircraft and missile manufacturer)
SAAF	South African Air Force
Sab	Sabbath
SABA	Scottish Amateur Boxing Association
SABC	South African Broadcasting Corporation
SABENA	*Societe anonyme belge d'exploitation de la navigation aerienne* = Belgian airline
SABRA	South African Bureau of Racial Affairs
SAC	Scientific Advisory Council; Scottish Autombile Club; State Athletics Commission (US)
SACEUR	Supreme Allied Commander, Europe (commands Nato armies)
SAD	Seasonal Affective Disorder
SADF	South African Defence Force
SADIE	scanning analogue-to-digital input equipment

SAE	stamped addressed envelope; self-addressed envelope; Society of British Automotive Engineers; Society of Automotive Engineers oil viscosity scale (US)
SAF	Strategic Air Force (US)
SAFE	South African Friends of England
S Afr	South Africa
SAG	Screen Actors' Guild (US)
SAGA	Social Amenities for the Golden Aged (British help and leisure organisation); Society of American Graphic Artists
SAGB	Spiritualist Association of Great Britain
SAH	Supreme Allied Headquarters
SAID	Sexual Allegations in Divorce
SAIDS	simian acquired immune deficiency syndrome
sal	salary
Salop	Shropshire
Sally Army	Salvation Army

S&M   SADISM AND MASOCHISM
SAUSAGES AND MASH

SALP	South African Labour Party
SALT	Strategic Arms Limitation Talks (US and former USSR)
Salv	Salvador
SAM	surface-to-air missile; sex appeal and magnetism
Sam	Samoa
S Am	South America
Samar	Samaritans
SAMH	Scottish Association for Mental Health
san	sanatorium; sanitary
s&d	song and dance
S&M, s&m	sadism and masochism, commonly sadomasochism; stock and machinery; sausages and mash
sand	sandwich
SANDS	Stillborn and Neonatal Death Society
Sane	Schizophrenia A National Emergency
S&F	stock and fixtures; shopping and fucking – a so-called genre of popular fiction featuring explicit sex scenes
S&FA	shipping and forwarding agents
S&H	shipping and handling charges
S&L	savings and loan association (US)
s&s	sex and shopping (popular fiction style)
SANR	subject to approval, no risk
SANROC	South African Non-Racial Olympics Committee
Sans	Sanskrit
sans	*sans* = without (eg *sans serif* is a typeface without serifs on the letters)
SAP	South African Police
sap	soon as possible (qv **asap**)
sapl	sailing as per (Lloyd's shipping) list
SAR	search and rescue; South African Republic;
Sar	Sarawak
SARAH	search and rescue homing (radar)
sarge	sergeant

sarl	*Societe a responsibilite limitee* = private limited company in France, Belgium, Switzerland and Luxembourg
SAS	Special Air Service; Scandinavian Airlines System; small astronomical satellite
SAT	scholastic aptitude test (US)
Sat	Saturday; Saturn
S At	South Atlantic
sat	satellite
SATB	soprano, alto, tenor and bass (choral music)
SATCO	signal automatic air traffic control system
sav	stock at valuation; sale at valuation
SAW	surface accoustic wave
sax	saxophone
SAYE	save as you earn
SB	small business; savings bank; Special Branch (Police political security department); sub-branch; stillborn
sb	single-breasted (suit style); stolen base (baseball)
SBA	School of Business Administration; standard beam approach (airports); sick-bay attendant
SBAC	Society of British Aerospace Companies
SBC	Schools Broadcasting Council; single board computer
SBD	silent but deadly (passing wind)
SBNO	Senior British Naval Officer
SBO	small bowel obstruction
SBS	sick-building syndrome; Special Boat Service
SBU	strategic business unit
SBV	seabed vehicle
SC	School Certificate (Aust and NZ); Signal Corps; Senior Counsel; Supreme Court; Special Constable; Star of Courage (Canada); Social Club; Staff Corps; Staff Captain; Schools Council
Sc	Scandinavia; Scotland; science; sculptor

sc	scale; sculptor; *sculpsit* = carved or engraved by; self-contained; small capitals (typesetting); science; scruple (weight)
SCA	Special Conservation Area; sickle-cell anemia (also **SCD**)
Scan	Scandinavia (also **Sc, Scand**)
s caps	small capitals (typesetting)
SCAR	Scientific (sometimes Special) Committee on Antarctic Research
Scarab	Submerged Craft Assisting Repair and Burial
SCB	Speedway Control Board; Solicitors Complaints Bureau
ScBC	Bachelor of Science (Chemistry)
ScBE	Bachelor of Science (Engineering)
SCBU	special care baby unit
SCC	Sea Cadet Corps
scc	single column centimetre (print advertising)
SCCAPE	Scottish Council for Commercial, Administrative and Professional Education
SCCL	Scottish Council for Civil Liberties
SCE	Scottish Certificate of Education
SCF	Save the Children Fund; Senior Chaplain to the Forces
SCG	Sydney Cricket Ground
SCGB	Ski Club of Great Britain
Sch	Schilling
sch	school; scholar; scholarship; schedule; schooner
sched	schedule (also **sch**)
schizo	schizophrenic
SCI	Scottish Central Institutions; Society of the Chemical Industry
sci	single column inch (print advertising)
SCID	severe combined immunodeficiency disease
sci-fi	science fiction
SCL	Scottish Central Library

SCLC	small cell lung cancer (carcinoma)		
SCM	State Certified Midwife		

An Abbreviated Quiz

Here are some abbreviations for various measurements. See if you can match the measurement with the item being measured.

1	22kt	**A**	light bulb
2	70dB	**B**	car engine
3	20in diag	**C**	gold ring
4	2B	**D**	can of drink
5	330ml	**E**	disturbing noise
6	100w	**F**	television set
7	4000rpm	**G**	load of coal
8	5cwt	**H**	pencil

(*Answers on page 163*)

SCOFF	Society for the Conquest of Flight Fear
SCOOP	Stop Crapping On Our Property (warning to dog owners)
SCOR	Scientific Committee on Oceanic Research
Scot	Scotland; Scottish; Scotsman
SCP	single-cell protein; Social Credit Party (Canada)
SCPS	Society of Civil and Public Servants
SCR	senior common room (universities); selective catalytic reactor
scr	script; scruple
Script	Scripture
SCS	space communications system; Soil Conservation Service (US)
SCSI	Small Computer System Interface ('scuzzy')
SCSS	Scottish Council of Social Service
SCU	Scottish Cycling Union; Scottish Cricket Union
scuba	self contained underwater breathing apparatus

SCOOP   STOP CRAPPING ON OUR PROPERTY

sculp	sculptor; sculpture
SCUM	Society for Cutting Up Men (a creation of Valeria Solanis who shot and wounded artist Andy Warhol in 1968)
SCV	*Stato della Citta del Vaticano* = Vatican City State
SCWS	Scottish Wholesale Cooperative Society
SD	standard deviation; Secretary of Defense (US); senile dementia; send direct; special delivery; special duty; State Department (US)
sd	same date; semi-detached; standard deviation (statistics); safe deposit; signed; said; sailed; sewed (bookbinding)
S/D	sight draft (banking)
SDA	Scottish Development Agency; Seventh Day Adventist
SDAT	senile dementia (Alzheimer type)
SDG	*Soli Deo Gloria* = Glory to God Alone
SDI	Strategic Defense Initiative (US 'Star Wars' project)
SDLP	Social Democratic and Labour Party (Ulster)
SDMJ	September/December/March/June: traditional months for quarterly repayments
SDO	senior duty officer
SDP	Social Democratic Party; social, domestic and pleasure (insurance)

SDRs	special drawing rights (banking)
SDS	scientific data system; strategic defense system (US)
SE	Stock Exchange (also **S/Ex, S/E**); South Eastern; Standard English
se	standard error (statistics); single-engined; single entry
SEAC	South East Asia Command; School Examination and Assessment Council
SEAF	Stock Exchange automatic exchange facility
SEAL	sea-air-land (US Military)
SEAQ	Stock Exchange automated quotations
SEATO	South East Asia Treaty Organisation
SEB	Former Southern Electricity Board
SEC	Securities and Exchange Commission (US)
sec	secretary; second; sector; seconded; section
SECAM	*sequential couleur a memoire* = French standard television broadcasting system
SECC	Scottish Exhibition and Conference Centre
Sec Gen	Secretary-General
secy	secretary
SED	Scottish Education Department; shipper's export declaration
SEDAR	submerged electrode detection and ranging
SEE	Society of Environmental Engineers
SEEA	*Societe europeenne d'energie atomique* = European Atomic Energy Society
Seeboard	Former South-Eastern Electricity Board
SEF	Shipbuilding Employers' Federation
seg	segment; segregate; segue
SEH	St Edmund Hall, Oxford University
Sel	Selwyn College, CambridgeUniversity
sel	select; selected; selection
SELNEC	South-East Lancashire and North-East Cheshire
SEM	scanning electron microscopy

Sem	Semitic
sem	seminary; semester (US); semicolon
semi	semi-detached house
SEN	special educational needs; State Enrolled Nurse
Sen	Senate; Senator
sen	senior (also **sr, snr**)
Sen M	Senior Master; **Sen Mist** = Senior Mistress
senr	senior (also **sen, sr, snr**)
SEO	senior executive officer
sep	separate; separation; sepal (botany)
Sept	September (also **Sep**)
seq	sequel; sequence; *sequens* = the following one; **seqq** = *sequentia* = the following ones
ser	series; serial; sermon; service; servant; service
Serb	Serbian
SERC	Science and Engineering Research Council

Abbreviated Quiz Answers

1 - C;   **2** - E;   **3** - F;   **4** - H;   **5** -D;   **6** - A;   **7** - B;   **8** - G

SERPS	State Earnings-Related Pension Scheme
SERT	Society of Electronic and Radio Technicians
serv	service; servant
SES	Stock Exchange of Singapore; **SESI** = Stock Exchange of Singapore Index
SET	Former selective employment tax (abandoned 1973)
SETI	search for extraterrestrial intelligence
17th Amendment	US constitutional amendment requiring senators to be elected by popular vote (1913)
17th Congress	USSR Congress that admitted widespread protests over rural collectivisation (1934)
17th Parallel	UN-agreed boundary between North and South Vietnam (1954)
sew	sewer; sewage; sewerage

SF	Sinn Fein; Society of Friends; science fiction; San Francisco; senior fellow; signal frequency; standard frequency; special forces
sf	science fiction; *sub finem* = towards the end; signal frequency
SFA	Scottish Football Association; sweet Fanny Adams = nothing
SFC	specific fuel consumption
Sfc	Sergeant first-class (US)
SFI	*Societe Financiere Internationale* = French International Finance Corporation
SFL	Scottish Football League; sequenced flashing lights (airports)
SFO	Serious Fraud Office; Superannuation Funds Office; Senior Flag Officer
SFOF	space flight operations facility (Nasa)
SFr	Swiss franc
SFU	suitable for upgrade (airline ticketing)
SG	Secretary General; Solicitor General; Scots Guards; senior grade; Stanley Gibbons (postage stamp identification number); Society of Genealogists; Surgeon General
sg	specific gravity
sgd	signed
SGF	Scottish Grocers' Federation
SGHWR	steam-generating heavy-water reactor
sgl	single
SGM	Sea Gallantry Medal
SGML	Standard generalized Markup Language
Sgt	Sergeant; **Sgt Maj** = Sergeant Major
SGU	Scottish Golf Union
SH	schoolhouse; scrum half (rugby); showers; Southern Hemisphere; Schleswig-Holstein
sh	second hand (also **s/h**); shilling; share (also **shr**); sheep; sheet; sacrifice hit (baseball)
SHA	Scottish Hockey Association; sidereal hour angle

SHAC	Shelter Housing Aid Centre
SHAEF	Supreme Headquarters Allied Expeditionary Forces (under Gen Eisenhower, London, WW2)
Shak	Shakespeare (also **Sh, Shake**)
SHAZAM!	Reputedly the combined powers of Solomon, Hercules, Atlas, Zeus, Achilles and Mercury
shd	should
Shef	Sheffield (also **Sheff**)
SHF	superhigh frequency
SHM	Society of Housing Managers
SHMO	Senior Hospital Medical Officer
SHO	Senior House Officer
sho	shutout (baseball)
shorts	short-term bonds; short-dated securities (investing)
SHP	single-flowered hardy perennial (horticulture)

That's Show Business!

The *Gong Show* was perhaps the most successful long-running talent show on US television. Some of the performers *were* talented but many were not, and it was their embarrassingly eye-wincing acts that made the show famous. Also famous were the secret abbreviations devised by the show's host, Chuck Barris, to describe some of the performers. Here are three that became public knowledge:

DAAR	dumb as a rock
VOAPE	victim of a pizza explosion (zits)
TWT	totally without talent

shpg	shipping
shpt	shipment
shr	share; shower
Shrops	Shropshire
SHS	*Societatis Historicae Socius* = Fellow of the Historical Society
SHT	single-flower hybrid tea (rose growing)

'shun	attention!
SHW	safety, health and welfare
SI	Most Exalted Order of the Star of India; Staten Island; seriously ill; sum insured
SI unit	*Systeme International d'Unites* = system of international units (eg ampere, metre, kilogram, kelvin, second etc)
SIA	Society of Investment Analysts; Spinal Injuries Association
SIB	Special Investigation Branch (Police); Savings and Investment Bank; Securities and Investment Board; self-injurious behaviour
Sib	Siberia
SIC	Standard Industrial Classification
Sic	Sicily; Sicilian
SICAV	*Societe d'investissement a capital variable* = unit trust
SID	*Spiritus in Deo* = His/Her spirit is with God; Society for International Development
SIDA	The AIDS acronym in French, Spanish and Italian
SIDS	sudden infant death syndrome (cot death)
SIF	stress intensity factor (engineering)
SIG	special interest group
Sig	*Signor* = Mr; *Signore* = Sir (Italian)
sig	signature; signal; signifies
SII	*Societe internationale de la lepre* = International Leprosy Association
SIM	self-inflicted mutilation; survey information on microfilm; *Societe internationale de musicologie* = International Musicological Society
SIMA	Scientific Instrument Manufacturers' Association
SIMC	*Societe internationale pour la musique contemporaine* = International Society for Contemporary Music
SIMCA	*Societe industrielle de mechanique et carosserie automobiles* = French car manufacturer
SIMD	single instruction, multiple data (computers); qv **SISD**

sing	singular
SIO	Senior Intelligence Officer
SIS	Security Intelligence Service (MI6)
sis	sister
SISD	single instruction, single data (computers); qv **SIMD**
SISTER	Special Institutions for Scientific and Technological Education and Research
SIT	Society of Industrial Technology
sit rep	situation report
sit rm	sitting room
SITA	Students' International Travel Association
sitcom	situation comedy (type of television programme)
SI unit	qv under **SI**
sit vac	situation vacant; **sits vac** = situations vacant
SIV	simian immunodeficiency virus
SIW	self-inflicted wound; qv **SIM**
16th Amendment	US constitutional amendment that introduced Federal income tax (1913)
$64,000 question	The essential question
SJ	Society of Jesus (Jesuits)
sj	*sub judice* = under judicial consideration
SJAA	St John Ambulance Association
SJAB	St John Ambulance Brigade
SJC	Supreme Judicial Court (US)
sk	sketch
SKC	Scottish Kennel Club
S Ken	South Kensington
SKF	*Svenska Kullagerfabriken* = Swedish steelmaking organisation
SKr	Swedish Krona
SL	sea level; Second Lieutenant, solicitor-at-law; scout leader; Squadron Leader; short lengths
sl	sleep; sleet; *sine loco* = without place of publication (bibliography)
SLA	Scottish Library Association; special landscape area

SLADE	Society of Lithographic Artists, Designers, Engravers and Process Workers
SLAET	Society of Licensed Aircraft Engineers and Technologists
SLAS	Society for Latin American Studies
Slav	Slavonic
SLBM	submarine-launched ballistic missile
SLCM	sea-launched cruise missile
SLD	Social and Liberal Democrats; specific learning difficulty
sld	sailed; sealed; sold; self-locking device
S Ldr	Squadron Leader
SLI	specific language impairment
SLLW	solid low-level waste (radioactive material); also **SLW**
SLO	Senior Liaison Officer
SLP	Scottish Labour Party; Socialist Labor Party (US)
SLR	single lens reflex (camera)
SLS	sodium lauryl sulphate (detergents)
SLSC	surf life saving club
SLTA	Scottish Licensed Trade Association
SLV	standard (or space) launch vehicle
SM	sales manager; stage manager; Sergeant Major; station master; silver medallist; Society of Miniaturists; stipendiary magistrate; Sons of Malta; Sisters of Mercy; strategic missile; sado-masochism
sm	small
SMAC	Standing Medical Advisory Committee
SMATV	satellite master antenna television
SMAW	shielded metal arc welding
SMBA	Scottish Marine Biological Association
SMBG	self-monitoring blood glucose (diabetes check)
SMC	Scottish Mountaineering Club; Small Magellanic Cloud (astronomy); standard mean chord
sm caps	small capitals (typesetting)

Smersh

SMERSH was not an Ian Fleming invention for his James Bond spy novels, but a real department of Russian Intelligence which had the motto, *SMERt SHpionen*, or "death to spies". It's most famous victim was Leon Trotsky, assassinated in 1940.

SMetO	Senior Meteorological Officer
SMHD	The Worshipful Company of Spectacle Makers' Higher Diploma in Ophthalmic Optics
SMIA	Sheet Metal Industries Association
SMJ	Sisters of Mary and Joseph
SMO	Senior Medical Officer
SMP	statutory maternity pay
SMPS	Society of Master Printers in Scotland
SMPTE	Society of Motion Picture and Television Engineers (US)
SMR	standard metabolic rate
SMTA	Scottish Motor Trade Association
SMTP	Simple Mail Transfer Protocol
SMW	standard metal window
SN, sn	serial number; service number; shipping note (also **S/N**); snow
S/N ratio	signal to noise ratio; **S/N curve** = stress number curve

Snafu and beyond

"Confusion or chaos regarded as the normal state" is how *Collins English Dictionary* defines this unusual-looking word. It is in fact an acronym for "situation normal, all fucked/fouled up" with WW2 British Army origins and thought to have derived from a common prewar abbreviation, MFU (military fuck up). Since the war **snafu** has become a commonplace noun denoting incredibly complex and avoidable confusion with no one in control and no remedial action in sight ("A trailer went under a low viaduct and, getting stuck, snarled traffic on four main routes. The snafu occurred at Markwood, off

Queens Boulevard" *–New York Daily News*). However there appear to be chaos scenarios that transcend even the most horrific snafus, calling for even more vivid acronyms of which these are a selection: **fubar** (fucked up beyond all recognition); **sapfu** (surpassing all previous fuck-ups); **cummfu** (complete utter monumental military fuck-up) and **tuifu** (the ultimate in fuck-ups).

SNB	sellers no buyers
SNCF	*Societe nationale des chemins de fer francais* = French National Railways
snd	sound
SNF	strategic nuclear forces; spent nuclear fuel; solids, not fat
SNFU	Scottish National Farmers' Union
SNG	substitute natural gas
SNH	Scottish National Heritage
SNIG	sustainable non-inflationary growth
SNLR	services no longer required
SNOBOL	string oriented symbolic language (computers)
SNP	Scottish National Party
SNPA	Scottish Newspaper Proprietors' Association
SNR	Society for Nautical Research; signal to noise ratio (also **S/N ratio**)
Snr, snr	Senior (also **Sr**)
Snr	*Senor* = Mr (in Spanish); also **Sr**
Snra	*Senhora* = Mrs (in Portuguese)
Snra	*Senora* = Mrs (in Spanish); also **Sra**
Snrta	*Senhorita* = Miss (in Portuguese)
Snrta	*Senorita* = Miss (in Spanish)
SO	Scottish Office; Senior Officer; Scientific Officer; Signal Officer; Staff Officer; Stationery Office; Symphony Orchestra
So	Southern
so, SO	selling order; shipping order; standing order; strike out
SOA	state of the art

SOAP	subjective, objective, analysis, planning (medical)
SOAS	School of Oriental and African Studies, London
SOB	silly old bastard; son of a bitch (N America)
SOC	Scottish Ornithologists' Club
Soc	Society; *società* = Italian company or partnership; Socrates
soc	social; society; socialist; sociology
Soc Dem	Social Democrat
sociol	sociology; sociologist
SOCO	scene-of-crime officer (police)
SOCONY	Standard Oil Corporation of New York
sod	sodium
SODOMEI	Japanese Federation of Trade Unions
SOE	Special Operations Executive (WW2)
SOED	Shorter Oxford English Dictionary
SOF	sound on film
SOFAA	Society of Fine Art Auctioneers
SOGAT	Society of Graphical and Allied Trades
SOHIO	Standard Oil Company of Ohio
SoHo	South of Houston Street (district in Manhattan); small office and home office (business description)
SOL	shit on the liver
Sol, sol	solicitor (also **Slr**); solution; soluble
SOLAS	Safety Of Life At Sea
Sol Gen	Solicitor General
solv	solvent
SOM	Society of Occupational Medicine
Som	Somerset
sonar	sound navigation and ranging
SOP	standard operating procedure
sop	soprano
Soph	Sophocles (Greek poet and dramatist)
soph	sophomore
SOR	sale or return
SOS	save our souls; the Morse code signal for distress

Sou	Southern; Southampton
Sov	Soviet; **Sov Un** = Soviet Union
sov	shut off valve; sovereign
Soweto	Southwestern Townships (Black African district in South Africa)
SP	Socialist Party; starting price (race betting); stop payment; supply point; *Summus Pontifex* = Supreme Pontiff, ie the Pope
Sp	Spain; Spanish; Spaniard; spring
sp	single phase (electrical); space; special; species; speed; sport; special position (advertising); spelling; specimen; spirit
SpA	*societa per azioni* (Italian public limited company)
spag	spaghetti
SpAm	Spanish American
Spam	spiced ham (proprietary brand of tinned meat)
Span	Spanish; Spaniard (also **Sp**)
SPANA	Society for the Protection of Animals in North Africa
SPARS	Women's Coast Guard Reserve (US) from s*emper Paratus* = always ready (WW2)
SPACT	South Pacific Air Transport Council
SPC	Society for the Prevention of Crime
SPCA	Society for the Prevention of Cruelty to Animals (US)
SPCK	Society for Promoting Christian Knowledge
SPD	*Sozialdemokratische Partei Deutschlands* = German Social Democratic Party; Salisbury Plain District
SPDA	single premium deferred annuity
SPE	Society of Petroleum Engineers
SPEC	South Pacific Bureau for Economic Cooperation
spec	specification; special; specimen; speculation; **specs** = specifications; spectacles
SPECTRE	Special Executive for Counter Intelligence, Revenge and Extortion, the fanciful terrorist organisation in Ian Fleming's James Bond novels

172

SPF	sun protection factor (effectiveness of sun-screen products)
SPG	Society for the Propagation of the Gospel
SPGA	Scottish Professional Golfers' Association
SPGB	Socialist Party of Great Britain
sp gr	specific gravity (also **sg**)
sp ht	specific heat
SpLD	special learning difficulties (education)
SPNC	Society for the Promotion of Nature Conservation
SPO	senior press officer
SPOD	Sexual Problems of the Disabled
SPOT	*Satellite Pour l'observation de la Terre* = series of French reconnaissance satellites; satellite positioning and tracking
SPQR	*Senatus Populusque Romanus* = the Senate and People of Rome; small profits, quick return
SPR	Society for Psychical Research
Spr	Spring
SPRINT	solid-propellant rocket-intercept missile
sprl	*societe de personnes a responsibilite limitee* = French private limited company
sptg	sporting
SPUC	Society for the Protection of the Unborn Child
Spurs	Tottenham Hotspur Football Club
SPVD	Society for the Prevention of Venereal Disease
sq	square; sequence
SQ	sick quarters; survival quotient
SQA	software quality assurance (computers)
Sqdn Ldr	Squadron Leader (also **Sq Ldr**)
sq cm	square centimetre
sq ft	square feet/foot
sq in	square inch
sq km	square kilometre
sq m	square metre
sq mi	square mile (also **sq m**)
sq mm	square millimetre

What's going to happen to SOS?

It is commonly believed that the distress call **SOS** is an acronym for 'Save Our Souls', or 'Save Our Ship'. In fact, it stands for three call letters of the Morse code (. . . - - - . . .): three dots(S), three dashes (O) and three dots (S), which were judged to be the easiest amd clearest to be sent by someone in dire distress. But 130 years after its first use in 1867 the Royal Navy has announced that in this age of secure communications Morse code is redundant and that training in it will be abandoned. Presumably, in the future, 'Mayday' (*m'aidez* = help me!) will take the place of SOS as the international shipping and aircraft distress call.

---

sqq	*sequentia* = the following ones (qv **seq, seqq**)
sq yd	square yard
SR	Saudi riyal; Seychelles rupee; self-raising (flour); Southern Region (railway); sodium ricinoleate (in toothpaste); Society of Radiographers; standard rate (taxation); synthetic rubber
S/R	sale or return (also **SOR**)
Sr	*Senhor* = Mr/Sir (Portuguese); *Senor* = Mr/Sir (Spanish); Senior
sr	short rate (finance); senior
SRA	Squash Rackets Association
Sra	*Senhora* = Mrs (Portuguese); *Senora* = Mrs (Spanish)
SR&CC	strikes, riot and civil commotion (insurance)
SRAM	short range attack missile
SRC	Science Research Council; *sociedad regular colectiva* (Spanish partnership); Students' Representative Council; Swiss Red Cross
SRCN	State Registered Children's Nurse
S-R connection	stimulus-response connection (psychological unit of learning)
Srl	*societa a responsibilita limitata* = Italian private limited company

SRO	sold right out; standing room only; single room occupancy; self-regulatory organisation; Statutory Rules and Orders
SRP	State Registered Physiotherapist; suggested retail price
SRS	*Societatis Regiae Sodalis* = Fellow of the Royal Society
Srta	*Senhorita* = Miss (Portuguese); *Senorita* = Miss (Spanish)
SRU	Scottish Rugby Union
SS	*Schutzstaffel* = Nazi paramilitary organisation; Social Security; Secret Service; Secretary of State; steamship; Sunday school; stainless steel (also **ss**); standard size; Straits Settlements; surface to surface (missiles)
S/S	same size; silk screen
ss	short stop (baseball); stainless steel
SSA	Scottish Schoolmasters' Association; Social Security Administration (US); Society of Scottish Artists
SSAE	stamped, self-addressed envelope
SSAFA	Soldiers', Sailors' and Airmens' Families Association
SSAP	Statement of Standard Accounting Practice
SSC	*Societas Sanctae Crucis* = Society of the Holy Cross; Scottish Ski Club; Species Survival Commission
SSE	soapsuds enema
SSFA	Scottish Schools' Football Association
S/Sg	Staff Sergeant (also **SSgt**)
SSHA	Scottish Special Housing Association
SSI	site of scientific interest (qv **SSSI**)
SSM	surface to surface missile
SSN	severely subnormal; Standard Serial Number
SSP	statutory sick pay
ssp	sub-species
SSPCA	Scottish Society for the Prevention of Cruelty to Animals
SSRI	selective serotonin re-uptake inhibitor

SSS	Secretary of State for Scotland; sick sinus syndrome; standard scratch score (golf)
SSSI	site of special scientific interest (qv **SSI**)
SST	supersonic transport
SSTA	Scottish Secondary Teachers' Association
SSU	Sunday School Union
ST	Standard Time; speech therapist; spring tide; Summer Time; *The Sunday Times*
St	Saint; Strait; Street; Statute
st	stanza; statement; street; strait; stet ('let it stand', in printing); stone (14lbs weight); stumped (in cricket); stitch (knitting)
STA	Swimming Teachers' Association; Sail Training Association
sta	station; stationery
stab	stable; stabilise; stabiliser
Staffs	Staffordshire
STAGS	Sterling Transferable Accruing Government Securities
stand	standard (also **std**); standardised
St And	St Andrews, Scotland
START	Strategic Arms Reduction Talks
stat	statistic; **stats** = statistics; statue; stationery
Stat Hall	Stationers' Hall, London
stbd	starboard
STC	Samuel Taylor Coleridge (English poet); Satellite Test Centre (US); State Trading Corporation (India); Sydney Turf Club; Standard Telephones and Cables Ltd
STD	subscriber trunk dialling; sexually transmitted disease
STE	Society of Telecom Executives
Ste	*Sainte* = Saint (fem)
Ste	*societe* = Co = French company
STEL	short-term exposure limit (radiation levels)
STEM	scanning transmission electron microscope

Sten	WW2 sub-machine gun invented by Shepherd and Turner of Enfield, England
sten	stenographer (also **steno**)
STEP	Special Temporary Employment Programme
ster	stereotype; sterling (also **Stg, £Stg**)
stg, Stg	sterling (also **Stlg, £stg, ster**)
stereo	stereophonic sound; stereophonic record player
St Ex	Stock Exchange
stge	stage; storage
STGWU	Scottish Transport and General Workers' Union
Sth, sth	South; southern (also **sthn**)
STI	*Straits Times* Index (Singapore Stock Exchange)
Stipe	Stipendiary Magistrate (also **Stip**)
Stir	Stirlingshire
stir, STIR	surplus to immediate requirements (qv **STR**)
stk	stock
STL	studio-to-transmitter link
STM	short-term memory
stn	station
STO	senior technical officer; standing order (also **S/O**)
STOL	short take-off and landing (aircraft)
STOLVCD	short take-off and landing, vertical climb and descent (aircraft)
STOP	Students Tired Of Pollution
STOPP	Society of Teachers Opposed to Physical Punishment
S to S	ship to shore; station to station
STP	scientifically treated petroleum; a mescaline type hallucinogenic drug
stp	standard temperature and pressure
STR, str	surplus to requirements (qv **STIR**)
str	straight; strait (also **Str**); structure; structural; strings (in music)
STRAC	strategic air command; strategic army corps (US)
STRAD	signal transmitting, receiving and distribution
Strad	Stradivarius (violin)
strep	streptococcus virus

STTA	Scottish Table Tennis Association
STUC	Scottish Trades Union Congress
stud	student
STV	Scottish Television Ltd; subscription television; standard test vehicle
stwy	stairway
SU	Scripture Union; strontium unit
Su	Sunday; Sudan
sub	subject; subscription; submarine; subsidiary; substitute; suburb; sub-editor; subsidy; subway
subd	subdivision
subj	subject (also **sub**)
Sub Lt	Sub-Lieutenant (also **Sub-Lt**)
subs	subscriptions
Suff	Suffolk
suff	sufficient; suffix
Sult	Sultan
sum	summer; summary
Sun	Sunday
SUNFED	Special United Nations Fund for Economic Development
SUNY	State University of New York
sup	superior; superfine; supply; supplement; supplementary; supreme
sup ben	supplementary benefit
superhet	supersonic heterodyne
supp	supplement; supplementary (also **sup, suppl**)
supr	supervisor
supt	superintendent
Sur	Surrey (also **Surr**)
sur	surface; surplus
surg	surgeon; surgery; surgical
Surr	Surrey
surr	surrender; surrendered; surrounds; surrounded; surrogate
surv	survey; surveyor; surveying; survived
Surv Gen	Surveyor General

SUS	Students' Union Society; Scottish Union of Students
susp	suspend; suspended
Suss	Sussex
SUT	Society for Underwater Technology
SV	safety valve (also **sv**); stroke volume (automotive); *Sancta Virgo* = Holy Virgin; *Sanctitas Vestra* = Your Holiness
sv	safety valve; side valve; sailing vessel; save (baseball); surrender value (also **s/v**)
SVD	swine vesicular disease
svg	saving (**svgs** = savings)
SVO	Scottish Variety Orchestra
svp	*s'il vous plait* = if you please
SVS	still camera video system
SW	southwest; southwestern; southwesterly; senior warden; South Wales; small woman (clothing); short wave; southwest London postcode (eg **SW10**)
Sw	Sweden; Swedish
sw	saltwater; seawater; seaworthy (also **s/w**); short wave; switch
SWA	South West Africa (now Namibia)
SWACS	space warning and control system
SWAG	scientific wild-assed guess
SWALK	sealed with a loving kiss
SWAPO	South West Africa People's Organisation
s/ware	software (computers)
SWAT	Special Weapons and Tactics (US police unit)
Swatch	Swiss watch (brand name)
SWB, swb	short wheel base
swbd	switchboard
swd	sewed (bookbinding)
SWEAT	Student Work Experience and Training (US career programme)
SWEB	South Wales Electricity Board (former)
Swed	Sweden; Swedish

SwF	Swiss franc
SWF	single white female
SWG	standard wire gauge
SWH	solar water heating
SWIE	South Wales Institute of Engineers
SWIFT	Society for Worldwide Interbank Financial Transmission
SWIMS	Study of Women in Men's Society (US)
Swing	sterling warrant into gilts (gilt-edged stock)
Switz	Switzerland
SWL	safe working load
SWLA	Society of Wildlife Artists
SWMF	South Wales Miners' Federation
SWOA	Scottish Woodland Owners' Association
SWOPS	single well oil production system
SWOT	strengths, weaknesses, opportunities, threats (formula used in marketing analysis of new products)
SWP	safe working pressure
SWRB	Sadler's Wells Royal Ballet (former)
SWWJ	Society for Women Writers and Journalists
Sx	Sussex
Sy	Sydney, New South Wales (also **Syd**)
S Yd	Scotland Yard
SYHA	Scottish Youth Hostels Association
syll	syllabus (also **syl**)
sym	symptom; symbol; symbolic; symmetrical; symphony; symphonic
symp	symposium
sync	synchronous; synchronise; synchronisation
syn	synonym; synthetic
synd	syndicate; syndicated
synop	synopsis
synth	synthetic; synthesiser
Syr	Syria
syr	syrup
syst	system; systematic

T

Truncated Words

When we use words like *cello, taxi, mob* and *zoo* we hardly think of them as abbreviations. But that is how they and many other short words began life – as truncated forms of longer words. At the turn of the century a well-to-do citizen might have ordered his servant to 'Call me a *taximeter cab*' (cab = cabriolet), but by 1907 he would have simply asked for a *taxi*. A *violoncello* became a *cello* in 1876 while a *zoological garden* had been a *zoo* for thirty years before. A *mob*, unsurprisingly, was cut away from the Latin mouthful *mobile vulgus* (= fickle populace) as early as 1688, and a good thing too!

The *Oxford English Dictionary* records hundreds of similar truncations, but the really interesting thing about them is that they have been around for much longer than we think:

ad	from *advertisement*	1841
bus	from *omnibus*	1832
flu	from *influenza*	1839
pants	from *pantaloons*	1840
phone	from *telephone*	1884
pro	from *professional*	1866
turps	from *turpentine*	1823
vet	from *veterinary surgeon*	1862

T   telephone; temperature; time; Tuesday; temporary; Territory; tenor; teacher; Trinity

t	table; tabulated; tabulation; taken; teaspoon(ful); tense; terminal; temperature; tenor; time; ton; tonne; town; troy (weight); turn
TA	telegraphic address; Territorial Army (former); table of allowances
T/A	technical assistant; temporary assistant
TAA	Territorial Army Association; Trans-Australia Airlines
TAB	Totalizator Agency Board (Aust and NZ); standard typhoid vaccine
tab	table; tabulate; tabulation; tablet
TAC	Tactical Air Command (US); Technical Assistance Committee (UN); Tobacco Advisory Committee; Trades Advisory Council
tach	tachometer
TACS	tactical air control system
TAI	*temps atomique international* = International Atomic Time
Tai	Taiwan
TAL	traffic and accident loss
Tal	*Talmud Tora*, Jewish laws and traditions
TALISMAN	Transfer Accounting Lodgement for Investors and Stock Management
tal qual	*talis qualis* = average quality
TAM	television audience measurement; tactical air missile
Tam	Tamil
Tamba	Twins and Multiple Births Association
tan	tangent
T&A	tits and ass (used to describe certain magazines and tabloid newspapers); tonsils and adenoids
t&b	top and bottom
T&CPA	Town and Country Planning Association
T&E, t&e	test and evaluation; tired and emotional (ie, drunk)
t&g	tongued and grooved (timber)

t&o	taken and offered (betting)
t&p	theft and pilferage
t&s, T&S	toilet and shower (real estate); transport and supply
T&T	Trinidad and Tobago
TANS	terminal area navigation system
TAO	Technical Assistance Operations (UN)
TAP	*Transportes Aeros Portugueses* = Portuguese Airlines
TAPS	Trans-Alaska Pipeline System
TAR	terrain-avoidance radar
Tarmac	bituminous surfacing (tar + John McAdam, pioneering roadmaker)
tarp	tarpaulin
TAS	true air speed (aircraft)
Tas	Tasmania
TASS	*Telegrafmpye Agentsvo Sovetskovo Soyuza* = Russian Press Agency
TAT	transatlantic telephone cable; thematic apperception test (psychology)
TATT	tired all the time (also **TAT**). A vague but medically recognised stress disorder
Tatts	Tattersall's (Australian lottery company)
TAURUS	Transfer and Automated Registration of Uncertified Stock
t-a-v	*tout-a-vous* = yours, ever (correspondence)
TAVR	Territorial and Army Volunteer Reserve (former)
tax	taxation
TB	torpedo boat; Treasury Bill; trial balance; tuberculosis
tb	true bearing (navigation); total bases (baseball)
TBA, tba	to be announced; tyres, batteries and accessories
tb&s	top, bottom and sides
TBCEP	tribetachlorethyl phosphate (fire retardant)
tbcf	to be called for
tbd	to be decided/determined
TBI	total body irradiation
T-bill	Treasury bill
TBL	through bill of lading

TBM	temporary benchmark; tactical ballistic missile; tunnel boring machine
TBO, tbo	total blackout (theatres); time between overhauls (aircraft)
T-bond	Treasury bond
TBS	training battle simulation; tight building syndrome
tbs	tablespoon; tablespoonsful (also **tbsp**)
TBT	tributyle tin (ingredient in marine paint)
TC	technical college; temporary clerk; town clerk; training centre; Trinity College; tennis club; temporary constable; Transport Command; tungsten carbide; twin carburettors
tc	temperature control; terra cotta; traveller's cheque; till cancelled; true course
TCA	tricyclic antidepressant (drug); trichloracetic acid (herbicide)
TCA cycle	tricarboxylic acid cycle (series of biochemical reactions)
TCAS	Threat Alert and Collision Avoidance System (aeronautics)
TCB	Thames Conservancy Board; take care of business
TCBM	transcontinental ballistic missile

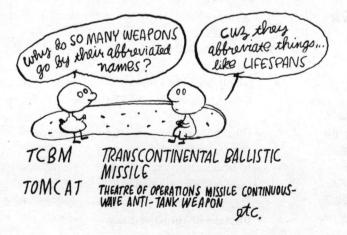

why do SO MANY WEAPONS go by their abbreviated names?

cuz they abbreviate things... like LIFESPANS

TCBM — TRANSCONTINENTAL BALLISTIC MISSILE

TOMCAT — THEATRE OF OPERATIONS MISSILE CONTINUOUS-WAVE ANTI-TANK WEAPON *etc.*

TCC	Trinity College, Cambridge; Transport and Communications Commission (UN)
TCCB	Test and County Cricket Board
TCD	Trinity College, Dublin
T-cell	T-lymphocyte
TCDD	tetrachlorodibenzodioxin (environmental pollutant)
TCE	trichlorethylene (solvent and anaesthetic)
TCF	time correction factor; Touring Club of France
TCGF	T-cell (lymphocyte) growth factor
tchr	teacher
TCI	Touring Club of Italy
TCM	Trinity College of Music, London (also **TCL**)
TCO	Trinity College, Oxford
TCP	trichlorophenylmethyliodisalicyl (antiseptic)

He got as far as "GIVE ME TRICHLOROPHENYLMETHYLIODISALICY...." then he died.

TCP TRICHLOROPHENYLMETHYLIODISALICY L

TCPA	Town and Country Planning Association
TD	Teaching Diploma; technical drawing; *Teachta Dala* = member of the Irish *Dail*; Territorial Decoration; Tilbury Docks; Treasury Department; trust deed; Tunisian dinar

td	technical data; test data; touchdown (American football)
TDB	*temps dynamique barycentrique* = barycentric dynamic time
TDC	Temporary Detective Constable
tdc	top dead centre (engineering)
TDG	twist drill guage
T-DNA	transferred deoxyribonucleic acid
TDO	tornado (meteorology)
TDRS	tracking and data relay satellite system
TDS	tabular data stream (computers)
TE, te	thermal efficiency; trace element; transverse electric; twin-engined (also **t/e**); trailing edge
TEA	terminal education age (age at which individuals leave school, college or university)
TEAC	Technical Education Advisory Council
TEC	Training and Enterprise Council; thermal expansion coefficient
tec, 'tec	detective
tech	technical; technology; technician; technique
TEF	toxicity equivalence factor
TEFL	teaching English as a foreign language
teg	top edge gilt (bookbinding)
Teh	Tehran
TEL	tetraethyl lead (petrol additive)
tel	telephone; telegram; telegraphic (also **tele, teleg**)
telex	teleprinter exchange
telly	television; television receiver
TELNET	teletype network (computers)
tel no	telephone number
TEM	transmission electron microscopy; transverse electromagnet; Territorial Efficiency Medal
temp	temperature; temporary; temporal; *tempore* = in the time of
Templar	tactical expert mission planner

ten	tenant; tenor
TENS	transcutaneous electrical nerve stimulation
TEPP	tetraethyl pyrophosphate (pesticide)
ter, terr	terrace; territory; territorial
TERCOM	terrain contour mapping
term	terminal; terminate; termination; terminology
tert	tertiary
TES	*The Times Educational Supplement*; thermal energy storage
Tesco	T E Stockwell and Sir John Cohen, supplier and founder of the supermarket chain
TESL	teacher of English as a second language
Tessa	Tax Exempt Special Savings Account
test	testimony; testimonial; testament; testator; testatrix
T-et-G	*Tarn-et-Garonne* = French department north of Haute Garonne
Tex-Mex	Texan-Mexican (cuisine)
text	textile
TF, tf	tax free; thin film (**TFR** = thin film transistor); *travaux forces* = hard labour (prison sentence)
TFA	Tenant Farmers' Association; total fatty acids
tfr	transfer
TG	Tate Gallery, London; thank God!; transformational grammar; Translators' Guild
tg	type genus
TGAT	Task Group on Assessment and Testing (Education)
TGB	*Tres Grande Bibliotheque* = planned new French National Library
TGI	Target Group Index
TGIF	Thank God it's Friday
TGT	turbine gas temperature
tgt	target
TGV	*train a grande vitesse* = French high speed passenger train

TGWU	Transport and General Workers' Union
TH	Trinity House, London (**TLWM** = Trinity House Low Water Mark; **THWM** = Trinity House High Water Mark); town hall; *Technische Hochschule* = German technical college
Th	Thursday; Theatre
th	hyperbolic tangent; thermal
Thai	Thailand; a citizen of Thailand
ThB	Bachelor of Theology
THC	tetrahydrocannabinol (active agent in cannabis)
THD	total harmonic distortion
ThD	Doctor of Theology
theol	theology; theological
theor	theory; theorem
therm	thermometer
THES	*The Times Higher Education Supplement*
THF	Trust-house Forte
THI	temperature-humidity index
tho, tho'	though
thoro	thoroughfare
thou	thousand
THR	total hip replacement
3i	Investors In Industry
3M	Minnesota Mining and Manufacturing Company (US)
3Rs	readin', 'ritin' and 'rithmetic
thro, thro'	through (also **thru** in the US)
Thur	Thursday
TI	Texas Instruments Corporation (US); thermal imaging; technical inspection
T/I	target indicator / identification
TIA	Tax Institute of America; transient ischemic attack (stroke)
Tib	Tibet; Tibetan
TIBOR	Tokyo Inter-bank Offered Rate

TIC	taken into consideration; total inorganic carbon; tourist information centre
TIF	*Transports Internationaux par Chemin de Fer* = International Railway Transport; telephone interference
TIFF	tagged image file format
TIGR	Treasury Investment Growth Receipts (bonds)
TIG welding	tungsten inert gas welding
TILS	Technical Information and Library Service
TIM	time is money; transient intermodulation distortion
timp	timpani
TIMS	The Institute of Management Sciences
TIN	taxpayer identification number
tinct	tincture
TIO	Technical Information Officer
TIR	*transport international des marchandises par la route* = European 26-country agreement allowing road trucks to bypass frontier customs until reaching their final destination
TIRC	Tobacco Industry Research Committee
TIROS	television and infrared observation satellite
TIS	technical information service
'tis	it is
tit	title; titular
TJ	triple jump (athletics)
Tk	Bangladeshi taka (monetary unit)
TKO, tko	technical knockout (boxing)
tks	thanks (also **thnks**)
tkt	ticket
TL	thermoluminescence; transmission line; Turkish lira
T/L	total loss; time loan; trade list
TLC	tender loving care (but also 'total lack of concern'!); total lung capacity; Trades and Labour Council (Australia)

tld	tooled (bookbinding)
TLO	Technical Liaison Officer
TLR	twin lens reflex (camera)
tlr	tailor; teller; trailer
TLS	*The Times Literary Supplement*
TLs	typed letter, signed
TM	trademark; transcendental meditation; Their Majesties; technical memorandum; tone modulation; transverse magnetic; tropical medicine; true mean (also **tm**)
TMA	Theatrical Management Association; Trans-Mediterranean Airways
T-men	US Treasury law enforcement agents
tmbr	timber
TMJ	temporomandibular joint dysfunction
TML	three mile limit (shipping); tetramethyl lead
TMS	temporomandibular syndrome
TMV	tobacco mosaic virus; true mean value
TN	true north
tn	telephone number; ton; tonne; town; train; transportation
T-note	Treasury note (in US)
TNP	*Theatre National Populaire* = French national theatre
TNT	2-4-6 trinitrotoluene (explosive)
T-number	total light transmission number (cameras)
TO	take off; turn over (also **t/o**); telegraphic order; technical officer; transport officer
T/O	turnover (also **t/o**)
TOB	temporary office building
ToB	Tour of Britain (cycling race)
tob	tobacco
TocH	Christian help organisation founded in 1915 by the Rev 'Tubby' Clayton. **Toc** = old Army signal for the letter **T**, for Talbot House, the movement's headquarters in London

TOD	time of delivery; The Open Door (organisation for phobia sufferers)
TOE	theory of everything
TOET	test of elementary training
Tok	Tokyo
TOL	Tower of London
TOM	*territoire d'outre mer* = French overseas territory
tom	tomato
TOMCAT	Theatre of Operations Missile Continuous-wave Anti-tank Weapon
TOMS	Total Ozone Mapping Spectrometer
TON	total organic nitrogen
tonn	tonnage
TOP	temporarily out of print
TOPIC	Teletext Output Price Information Computer
topog	topography
TOPS	Training Opportunities Scheme
Tor	Toronto
torn	tornado
torp	torpedo
TOS	temporarily out of service/stock
Toshiba	Tokyo Shibaura Electrics Corporation
tot	total
tote	totalisator
TOTP	Top of the Pops (TV programme)
tour	tourist; tourism
tourn	tournament (also **tourney**)
tox	toxicology; toxicologist (also **toxicol**)
TP, tp	taxpayer; to pay; test panel; town planner; title page; true position; third party; treaty port; *tout paye* = all expenses paid; *tempo primo* = at the original tempo; *tempore Paschale* = at Easter
TPC	Trade Practices Commission (Australia); The Peace Corps (US)
TPI	tax and price index; threads per inch; totally and permanently incapacitated

TPO	Tree Preservation Order; travelling post office
TPR	temperature, pulse and respiration
Tpr	Trooper
TPS	toughened polystyrene
tpt	trumpet
TQM	total quality management
TR	Territorial Reserve; *tempore regis/reginae* = in the time of the king/queen; test run; tracking radar; Theodore Roosevelt (US president); trust receipt
T/R	transmitter/receiver (also **TR** = transmit-receive)
tr	trace; track; tragedy; train; trainee; transaction; transfer; translate; translation; translator; transport; transpose; treasurer; truck; trust; trustee
trad	traditional (**trad jazz** = traditional jazz); *traduttore* = translator; *traduzione* = translation
TRADA	Timber Research and Development Association (also **TRDA**)
trag	tragedy
trannie	transistor radio
Trans	Transvaal
trans	transaction; transfer; transferred; transit; transitive; translated; translation; translator; transparent; transport; transpose (also **tr**); transverse
trav	travel; traveller
TRC	Thames Rowing Club; Tobacco Research Council
tr co	trust company
Trd	Trinidad (also **Trin**)
Treas	Treasury; Treasurer
TRF	tuned radio frequency (also **trf**)
trf	tariff
trg	training
TRH	Their Royal Highnesses
trib	tribal; tributary

Tribeca	Triangle Below Canal Street (New York City neighbourhood)
TRIC	trachoma inclusion conjunctivitis
trig	trigonometry; trigonometric
Trin	Trinidad; Trinity College (Oxford); Trinity Hall (Cambridge)
trip	tripos (final examination for Cambridge University honours degree)
TRM	trademark
TRNC	Turkish Republic of Northern Cyprus
TRO	temporary restraining order
trom	trombone (also **tromb**)
trop	tropical (**trop med** = tropical medicine)
trs	transfer; transpose
TRSB	time reference scanning beam
TRSR	taxi and runway surveillance radar
TS	Television Society; Theosophical Society; Tourette's syndrome; training ship; Treasury Solicitor; test summary; tough shit
ts, TS	tensile strength; till sale; twin screw; typescript; temperature switch
TSA	time series analysis; total surface area
TSB	Trustee Savings Bank
TSE	Tokyo Stock Exchange; Toronto Stock Exchange; transmissible spongiform encephalopathy
TSgt	Technical Sergeant
TSH	thyroid stimulating hormone (thyrotropin)
TSO	Trading Standards Officer
tsp	teaspoon; teaspoonful
TSR	tactical strike reconnaissance; Trans-Siberian Railway
TSS	toxic shock syndrome; time-sharing system; twin screw steamship
TSSA	Transport Salaried Staff's Association
TSU, tsu	this side up
tsvp	*tournez s'il vous plait* = please turn over

TT	Tourist Trophy (Isle of Man TT motorcycle races); technical training; teetotaller; telegraphic transfer; tetanus toxoid; Trust Territories; tuberculin-tested (milk)
TTA	Travel Trade Association
TTC	teachers' training course; Technical Training Command
TTF	Timber Trade Federation
TTFN	Ta-ta for now (catchphrase of 1940s radio star Tommy Handley, and later of American TV comedy character Sergeant Bilko)
TTL, ttl	through-the-lens (cameras); transistor-transistor logic
TTT	Tyne Tees Television Ltd, Newcastle upon Tyne; team time trial
TTTC	Technical Teachers' Training College
TU	trade union; thermal unit; transmission unit; Tupolev (range of Russian aircraft, eg supersonic **TU-144**)
Tu	Tuesday (also **Tue**)
TUAC	Trade Union Advisory Committee
tub	tubular
TUC	Trades Union Congress
TUCC	Transport Users' Consultative Committee
TUCGC	Trades Union Congress General Council
turb	turbine; turboprop
Turk	Turkey; Turkish
TURP	Transurethral resection of the prostate
turps	turpentine
TV, tv	television; television receiver; test vehicle; terminal velocity
TVA	Tennessee Valley Authority (US); *taxe a la valeur ajoutee* = French value added tax
TVP	textured vegetable protein
TVR	television rating (audience measurement)

TVRO	television receive only (antennae)
TW, tw	tail wind; travelling wave (TV antennae)
T/W	three-wheel (vehicle)
TWA	Thames Water Authority; Trans-World Airlines
'twas	it was
'twill	it will
'twixt	betwixt (archaic form of *between*)
TWN	teleprinter weather network
2,4,5-T	2,4,5-trichlorophenoxyacetic acid (herbicide)
TWOC	taking without owner's consent (police term for car theft); also **TAWOC** = taken away without owner's consent
TW3	*That Was The Week That Was* (1960s BBC satire programme)
TWU	Transport Workers' Union (US)
TYC	Thames Yacht Club; two-year-old course (racing)
TYO, tyo	two-year-old (racing)
typ	typical; typing; typist; typography; typographer
typh	typhoon
typo	typographical error; typography
typw	typewriter; typewritten

U

UIAA et al

There are scores of abbreviations beginning with the letters **UI**. In almost all cases these are international unions of like organisations abbreviated from the French title. **UIAA** for example is the *Union internationale des associations d'annonceurs*, which is the International Union of Advertisers' Associations. You are unlikely, in the normal course of events, to need intimate acquaintance with the vast majority of them, including the **UIEIS** (*Union internationale pour l'etude des insectes sociaux* = International Union for the Study of Social Insects) and perhaps the **UIMP** (*Union internationale pour la protection de la moralite publique* = International Union for Protecting Public Morality). If in doubt you could try calling the **UAI** in Paris – confusingly, not the **UIA**, the anglicised Union of International Associations – nor the **UAI** (*Union academique internationale* = International Union of Academies), nor the **UAI** (*Union astronomique internationale* = International Astronomical Union), but the *Union des associations internationales* = the aforesaid Union of International Associations, which supervises the whole shebang!

U	Universal Certificate (movies that may be seen by children unaccompanied by adults); university; united; unionist; upper class (as in **U** and **non-U** for acceptability); Burmese equivalent of Mr; you (as in **IOU** = I owe you); unit; unsatisfactory; urinal

u	unit; unsatisfactory; *und* = and
UA	United Artists Corporation (Hollywood); under age
U/a	underwriting account
UAA	United Arab Airlines
UAB	Universities Appointments Board
UAC	Ulster Automobile Club
UAE	United Arab Emirates
UAL	United Airlines
UAM	underwater-to-air missile
u&lc	upper and lower case (printing)
u&o	use and occupancy
UAOD	United Ancient Order of Druids (friendly society)
UAP	United Australia Party
UAR	United Arab Republic
UARS	upper atmosphere research satellite
UART	universal asynchronous receiver-transmitter
uas	upper airspace
UAU	Universities Athletic Union
UAW	United Automobile Workers (US)
UB	United Brethren
UB-40	Registration card issued to the unemployed
UBA	ultrasonic bone analysis
UBC	University of British Columbia
UBF	Union of British Fascists
U-boat	*unterseeboot* = submarine
UBR	Uniform Business Rate (tax); University Boat Race (annually, between Cambridge and Oxford)
UBS	United Bible Societies
UC	University College; urban council; under construction; under cover; uterine contraction
Uc	Film and video classification suitable for and of interest to children
uc	upper case (printing)
u/c	undercharged

UCA	United Chemists' Association
UCAE	Universities' Council for Adult Education
UCATT	Union of Construction, Allied Trades and Technicians
UCBSA	United Cricket Board of South Africa
UCC	Universal Copyright Convention; Union Carbide Corporation
UCCA	Universities Central Council on Admissions
UCD	University College, Dublin
UCH	University College Hospital, London
UCHD	usual childhood diseases (also **UCD**)
UCI	*Union cycliste internationale* = International Cyclists' Union; University of California at Irvine
UCL	University College, London
ucl, UCL	upper cylinder lubricant
UCLA	University of California at Los Angeles
UCM	University Christian Movement
UCMSM	University College and Middlesex School of Medicine
UCNW	University College of North Wales
UCR	unconditioned response (psychology)
UCS	University College School, London; unconditioned stimulus (psychology)
UCSB	University of California at Santa Barbara
UCSD	University of California at San Diego
UCSW	University College of South Wales
UCTA	United Commercial Travellers' Association (former)
UCW	Union of Communication Workers; University College of Wales
UD	United Dairies
UDA	Ulster Defence Association
UDC	Urban District Council; universal decimal classification; Urban Development Corporation; United Daughters of the Confederacy (US)
udc	upper dead centre (engineering)
UDCA	Urban District Councils' Association

UDF	Ulster Defence Force; United Democratic Front (South Africa)
UDI	Unilateral Declaration of Independence
UDM	Union of Democratic Mineworkers
UDP	United Democratic Party
UDR	Ulster Defence Regiment
UEA	University of East Anglia; Universal Esperanto Association
UED	University Education Diploma
UEFA	Union of European Football Associations
UER	university entrance requirements; *Union europeenne de radio-diffusion* = European Broadcasting Union; unsatisfactory equipment report
UF	United Free Church of Scotland (also **UFC**); urea formaldehyde
UFA	unsaturated fatty acid
UFC	University Funding Council
UFCW	United Food and Commercial Workers International (US)
UFF	Ulster Freedom Fighters
UFI	University for Industry
UFFI	urea formaldehyde foam insulation
UFO	unidentified flying object
UFTAA	Universal Federation of Travel Agents' Associations
UFU	Ulster Farmers' Union
u/g	underground
UGWA	United Garment Workers of America
UHF, uhf	ultra-high frequency
UHT, uht	ultra-high temperature; ultra-heat-treated (as for milk)
UHV, uhv	ultra-high voltage; ultra-high vacuum
U/I, u/i	under instruction
UJ	universal joint; union jack (**UJC** = Union Jack Club, London)
UK	United Kingdom

UK Postcodes

London, East	E	Durham	DH
London, East Central	EC	Edinburgh	EH
London, North	N	Enfield	EN
London, Northwest	NW	Exeter	EX
Aberdeen	AB	Falkirk	FK
Bath	BA	Galashiels	TD
Belfast	BT	Glasgow	G
Birmingham	B	Gloucester	GL
Blackburn	BB	Halifax	HX
Blackpool	FY	Harrowgate	HG
Bolton	BL	Harrow	HA
Bournemouth	BH	Hemel Hempstead	HP
Bradford	BD	Hereford	HR
Brighton	BN	Huddersfield	HD
Bristol	BS	Hull	HU
Bromley	BR	Ilford	IG
Canterbury	CT	Inverness	IV
Cardiff	CF	Ipswich	IP
Carlisle	CA	Kilmarnock	KA
Cambridge	CB	Kingston-upon-Thames	KT
Chelmsford	CM	Kirkcaldy	KY
Chester	CH	Kirkwall	KW
Cleveland	TS	Lancaster	LA
Colchester	CO	Leeds	LS
Coventry	CV	London, Southeast	SE
Crewe	CW	London, Southwest	SW
Croydon	CR	London, West	W
Darlington	DL	London, West Central	WC
Dartford	DA	Leicester	LE
Derby	DE	Lerwick	ZE
Doncaster	DN	Lincoln	LN
Dorchester	DT	Liverpool	L
Dudley	DY	Llandrindod Wells	LD
Dumfries	DG	Llandudno	LL
Dundee	DD	Luton	LU

Manchester	M	Southall	UB
Medway	ME	Southampton	SO
Milton Keynes	MK	Southend-on-Sea	SS
Motherwell	ML	Stevenage	SG
Newcastle upon Tyne	NE	Stoke-on-Trent	ST
Newport	NP	Stockport	SK
Northampton	NN	Sunderland	SR
Nottingham	NG	Sutton	SM
Norwich	NR	Swansea	SA
Oldham	OL	Swindon	SN
Oxford	OX	Taunton	TA
Paisley	PA	Telford	TF
Perth	PH	Tonbridge	TN
Peterborough	PE	Torquay	TQ
Plymouth	PL	Truro	TR
Portsmouth	PO	Twickenham	TW
Preston	PR	Wakefield	WF
Reading	RG	Walsall	WS
Redhill	RH	Warrington	WA
Romford	RM	Watford	WD
Sheffield	S	Wigan	WN
Salisbury	SP	Wolverhampton	WV
Shrewsbury	SY	Worcester	WR
Slough	SL	York	YO

UKAEA	United Kingdom Atomic Energy Authority
UKAPE	United Kingdom Association of Professional Engineers
UKBG	United Kingdom Bartenders' Guild
UKCOSA	United Kingdom Council for Overseas Students' Affairs
UKDA	United Kingdom Dairy Association
uke	ukulele
UKLF	United Kingdom Land Forces
UKOTS	United Kingdom Overseas Territories (formerly the unfortunately abbreviated **BOTS** = British Overseas Territories)

UKPA	United Kingdom Pilots' Association
Ukr	Ukraine
UL	university library; upper limb; upper limit
ULCC	ultralarge crude carrier (bulk oil)
ULF, ulf	ultra low frequency
ULM	ultrasonic light modulator; universal logic module
ULS, uls	unsecured loan stock
ULSEB	University of London School Examinations Board
ult	ultimate; ultimately; *ultimo* = during the previous month
um, u/m	unmarried
UMF	Umbrella Makers' Federation
UMFC	United Methodist Free Churches
UMi	Ursa Minor (**UMa** = Ursa Major)
UMIST	University of Manchester Institute of Science and Technology
ump	umpire
UMTS	Universal Mobile Telephone System
UN	United Nations

UN – The United Nations Family

The United Nations, an organisation that, like the EU after it, has begat a vast family of programmes, committees, commissions, administrations, consultancies and agencies.

Some, like **UNRRA** (1943-49) fulfilled their purpose and either merged with another agency or passed on. Of at least a hundred or so, here are a few that are worth knowing.

UNARCO	United Nations Narcotics Commission
UNCCP	United Nations Conciliation Commission for Palestine
UNCDF	United Nations Capital Development Fund
UNCIO	United Nations Conference on International Organisation
UNDP	United Nations Development Programme

UNDRO	United Nations Disaster Relief Organisation
UNEC	United Nations Education Conference
UNECA	United Nations Economic Commission for Asia
UNEDA	United Nations Economic Development Administration
UNEF	United Nations Emergency Force
UNEP	United Nations Environment Programme
UNESCO	United Nations Educational, Scientific and Cultural Organisation
UNFAO	United Nations Food and Agriculture Organisation
UNGA	United Nations General Assembly
UNIC	United Nations Information Centre
UNICEF	United Nations Children's Fund
UNIDO	United Nations Industrial Development Organisation
UNISCAT	United Nations Expert Committee on the Application of Science and Technology
UNO	United Nations Organisation
UNREF	United Nations Refugee Emergency Fund
UNRWA	United Nations Relief and Works Agency
UNSCC	United Nations Standards Coordinating Committee
UNSG	United Nations Secretary General
UNSR	United Nations Space Registry
UNWCC	United Nations War Crimes Commission

un	united; unified; union; unsatisfactory
unauth	unauthorised
UNB	universal navigation beacon
unclas	unclassified (also **unclass**)
UNCLE	United Network Command for Law Enforcement (from the fictional TV programme, *The Man from U.N.C.L.E*)
uncir	uncirculated (numismatics)
uncond	unconditional
uncor	uncorrected
undergrad	undergraduate
undtkr	undertaker

unexpl	unexplained; unexplored; unexploded
uni	university (also **univ**)
unif	uniform
Unit	Unitarian
UNITA	*Uniao Nacionale para a Independencia Total de Angola* = National Union for the Total Independence of Angola
UNIVAC	universal automatic computer
unkn	unknown
unm	unmarried
unop	unopened
UNP	United National Party (Sri Lanka)
unpd	unpaid
unpub	unpublished
unsat	unsaturated; unsatisfactory
uoc	ultimate operating capacity/capability
UOD	ultimate oxygen demand
UP	United Press; United Presbyterian; Union Pacific; University Press; Uttar Pradesh (India); Ulster Parliament; unsaturated polyester/polymer
up, u/p	underproof (alcoholic content)
UPA	United Productions of America (film studio)
UPC	universal product code (bar code); Universal Postal Convention
upd	unpaid
UPF	untreated polyurethane foam
UPGC	University and Polytechnic Grants Committee
uphol	upholstery
UPI	United Press International
UPNI	Unionist Party of Northern Ireland
UPOA	Ulster Public Officers' Association
UPR	unearned premiums reserve; Union Pacific Railroad (US)
UPS	United Parcel Service; uninterruptible power supply (computers)

UPU	Universal Postal Union
UPUP	Ulster Popular Unionist Party
UR	unconditoned reflex / response (psychology)
Ur	Uruguay; Urdu (also **Urd**)
URBM	ultimate range ballistic missile
URC	United Reformed Church
urg	urgent; urgently
URI	upper respiratory infection (**URTI** = upper respiratory tract infection)
URL	Unilever Research Laboratory; uniform resource locator
urol	urology; urologist
US	United States (**US66** = United States Highway Route 66); ultrasonic; ultrasound; Undersecretary; unconditioned stimulus
u/s, U/S	unserviceable; unsaleable
USA	United States of America
USA/ABF	United States of America Amateur Boxing Federation
USAC	United States Air Corps; United States Auto Club
USAEC	United States Atomic Energy Commission
USAF	United States Air Force
USAFE	United States Air Forces in Europe
USAID	United States Agency for International Development
USB	universal serial bus
USC	Ulster Special Constabulary; United Services Club; United States Congress; University of Southern California
USCG	United States Coast Guard
USDA	United States Department of Agriculture
USDAW	Union of Shop, Distributive and Allied Workers
usf	*und so fort* = and so on, etc (**usw** = und so weiter = and so forth)
USFL	United States Football League

USG	United States Government; United States Standard Gauge (railroads)
USGA	United States Golf Association
USgall	United States gallon
USGS	United States Geological Survey
USh	Uganda shilling
USIS	United States Information Service
USLTA	United States Lawn Tennis Association
USM	unlisted securities market; underwater-to-surface missile; United States Mail; United States Marines; United States Mint
USMA	United States Military Academy
USMC	United States Marine Corps
USN	United States Navy
USNA	United States Naval Academy
USNR	United States Naval Reserve
USO	United Service Organisation (US)
USP	unique selling proposition (advertising); United States patent (also **USPat**); United States Pharmacopeia
USPC	Ulster Society for the Preservation of the Countryside
USPG	United Society for the Propagation of the Gospel
USPO	United States Post Office (**USPS** = United States Postal Service)
USS	United States Ship/Steamship; Undersecretary of State; United States Senate; Universties Superannuation Scheme
USSR	Union of Soviet Socialist Republics
USTA	United States Tennis Association
usu	usual, usually
USVI	United States Virgin Islands
USW, usw	ultrashort wave
UT	unit trust; universal time; urinary tract; Union Territory (India)
ut	utility; user test

UTA	*Union de Transports Aeriens* (French airline); Ulster Transport Authority; Unit Trust Association
UTC	universal time coordinated
Utd	United
UTDA	Ulster Tourist Development Association
ute	utility (Australian pick-up truck)
U3A	University of the Third Age
UTI	urinary tract infection
UTS	ultimate tensile strength
UTWA	United Textile Workers of America
UU	Ulster Unionist
UUUC	United Ulster Unionist Council
UUUP	United Ulster Unionist Party
uuV	*unter ublichen Vorbehelt* = errors and omissions excepted
UV	ultraviolet (**UV-A** = radiation with wavelength of 320-380nm; **UV-B** = radiation with wavelength of 280-320nm)
UVAS	ultraviolet astronomical satellite
UVF	Ulster Volunteer Force
UVL	ultraviolet light
UW, uw	underwater; unladen weight
UWA	University of Western Australia
UWC	Ulster Workers' Council
UWIST	University of Wales Institute of Science and Technology (also **Uwist**)
UXB	unexploded bomb
Uz	Uzbekistan

V

The Versatile V

The letter **V** is probably the most commonly used initial and abbreviation, and is also of some antiquity: it still represents the Roman numeral 5. It also stands for dozens of words, symbols and names, from (in lower case) vacuum, valley and valve to vice, volcano and vowel; and from (in upper case) Venerable and Vicar to Viscount and Victoria the Queen. It also serves as the symbol for vanadium, velocity and volt, and identifies cars registered in Vatican City. With numerals added a **V-1** was a WW2 German robot bomb, a **V-2** was a rocket-powered missile, a **V8** is a car engine and a **V-sign** was Winston Churchill's two-finger salute to the enemy.

V	Venerable, Vice, Very (in titles); Viscount; the Roman numeral 5; *Via* = Italian street; Vicar; verb; volume; volt; voltmeter; Volunteer
v	vacuum; valley; vale; valve; vein; ventral; verb; verse; velocity; version; verso (printing and numismatics); versus; vertical; very; via; vide; vicarage; vice (in titles); village; violin; virus; visibility; vocative (grammar); voice; volcano; volume; *von* = Mr in German; vowel
V1, V-1	*Vergeltungswaffe* = WW2 German pulsejet robot bomb
V2, V-2	*Vergeltungswaffe* = WW2 German rocket-powered ballistic missile used to bombard London

V8	auto engine with eight cylinders arranged in V-formation (also **V2**, **V4**, **V6**, **V12** and **V16**)
VA	Royal Order of Victoria and Albert; value-added; Veterans' Administration (US); Voice of America (radio); value analysis
va	value analysis; verb active; viola
VABF	Variety Artists' Benevolent Fund
vac	vacant; vacancy; vacation; vacuum
vacc	vaccine; vaccination
VAD	Voluntary Aid Detachment (to the Red Cross)
VADAS	voice activated domestic appliance system
V-Adm	Vice-Admiral
vag	vagrant; vagrancy; vagina
val	valuation; valued; valley
valid	validation
Valpo	Valparaiso
van	advantage (tennis); vanguard; vanilla
Vanc	Vancouver
V&A	Victoria and Albert Museum, London
v&t	vodka and tonic
V&V, v&v	verification and validation (computers)
VAPI	visual approach path indicator (aeronautics)
vap prf	vapour proof
var	variable; variation; variant; variety; various; visual aural range (also **VAR**)
Varig	*Empresa de Viacao Aerea Rio Grandense* = Brazilian national airline (also **VARIG**)
varn	varnish
varsity	university
vas	vasectomy
VASARI	Visual Art System for Archiving and Retrieval of Images (computers)
vasc	vascular
VASI	visual approach slope indicator (aeronautics)
VAT	value added tax
Vat	Vatican
VATE	versatile automatic test equipment

vaud	vaudeville
VAV	variable air volume
VAWT	vertical axis wind turbine
vb	verb (**vbl** = verbal)
VBI	vertebronasilar insufficiency
V bomber	Class of UK bombers, eg Valiant, Vulcan, etc
VC	Victoria Cross; Vatican City; Vice-Chairman; Vice-Chancellor; Vice Consul; Vickers Commercial aircraft (eg **VC10** etc); Viet Cong; venture capital; vinyl chloride; vapour compression
vc	violoncello; cello; visual communication
VCA	vinyl carbonate
VCC	Veteran Car Club of Great Britain
VCCS	voltage controlled current source
VCE	variable-cycle engine
Vce	Venice
VCG	Vice Consul-General; vertical centre of gravity
VCM	vinyl chloride monomer (plastic)
VCO	voltage controlled oscillator
VCR	video casette recorder/recording; visual control room (airports)
Vcr	Vancouver
VD	venereal disease; vascular dementia
vd	void
V-Day	Victory Day (qv **VE Day, VJ Day**)
VDC	Volunteer Defence Corps
VDH	valvular disease of the heart
VDI	virtual device interface (computers)
VDP	*vin de pays* = quality French local wine (qv **VDQS, AOC**)
VDQS	*vins delimites de qualite superieure* = high quality French wine classification (qv **AOC, VDP**)
VDT	visual display terminal
VDU	visual display unit
VE Day	Victory in Europe Day (May 8, 1945)
veg	vegetables (also **veggies**), vegetarian; vegetation

veh	vehicle; vehicular
vel	vellum; velocity; velvet
Velcro	*velours* + *croche* = hooked velvet (Swiss-invented fastener)
Ven	Venerable; Venice; Venetian; Venus; Venezuela
ven	veneer; venereal; venison; ventral; ventricle; *vendredi* = Friday; venomous
vent	ventilation; ventriloquist
Ver	*Verein* = German company or association)
ver	version; verify; verification; verse; vermilion (also **verm**); vertical
VERA	versatile reactor assembly
verb et lit	*verbum et literatim* = word for word, letter for letter
verb sap	*verbum sapienti sat est* = a word is enough for the wise (also **verb sat**)
Verl	*Verlag* = publisher
verm	vermiculite
vern	vernacular
vers	version (also **ver**)
vert	vertebra; vertical
Very Rev	Very Reverend
vet	veterinary surgeon; veteran
Vet Admin	Veterans' Administration (US)
VetMB	Bachelor of Veterinary Medicine
vet sci	veterinary science
VF	video frequency; voice frequency
vf	very fair (weather); very fine (numismatics)
VFA	volatile fatty acid
VFM	value for money
VFR	visual flight rules (aeronautics)
VG	Vicar General; very good
vg	very good; *verbi gratia* = for example
VGA	video graphics array
vgc	very good condition
VH, vh	vertical height
VHC	very highly commended

VHD	video high density
VHF	very high frequency; very high fidelity
VHS	Video Home System (videotape standard)
VHT	very high temperature
VI	Virgin Islands; Vancouver Island; vertical interval; viscosity index; volume indicator
vi	*vide infra* = see below (also **vid**)
VIA	Visually Impaired Association
viad	viaduct
VIASA	*Venezolana Internacional de Aviacion* = Venezuela International Airways
vib	vibration; vibraphone
Vic	Victoria, Australian State
vic	vicar; vicarage; vicinity; victory
Vice-Adm	Vice-Admiral
vid	*vide* = see, refer to; video
vign	vignette
vil	village
VIN	vehicle identification number (US)
vini	viniculture
VIP	very important person

VIP   VERY IMPORTANT PERSON

VIR	*Victoria Imperatrix Regina* = Victoria, Empress and Queen
Vis	Viscount; Viscountess
vis	visible; visibility; visual
visc	viscosity
vit	vitreous
vit stat	vital statistics
viz	*videlicet* = namely
VJ Day	Victory over Japan Day (end of WW2, August 15, 1945)
VL	Vulgar Latin
vl	violin
vla	viola
Vlad	Vladivostok
VLB	vertical lift bridge
VLBC	very large bulk carrier
VLBW	very low birth weight
VLCC	very large crude carrier
VLF	very low frequency
VLLW	very low level waste (radioactivity)
vln	violin
VLR	very long range (aircraft)
VLS	vapour-liquid-solid
VLSI	very large scale integration (computers)
VM	Victory Medal; Virgin Mary; velocity modulation; virtual machine; volatile matter
VMC	visual meteorological conditions
VMD	Doctor of Veterinary Medicine
VMH	Victoria Medal of Honour (Royal Horticultural Society)
VMS	Voluntary Medical Services; virtual machine system (computers)
V-neck	V-cut neck in clothing
VO	voice over (in film-making, TV); Royal Victorian Order; valuation officer; very old (brandy, spirits); veterinary officer
vo	verso
VOA	Voice of America; Volunteers of America

VOC	volatile organic compound
voc	vocalist; vocation
vocab	vocabulary
vol	volume (**vols** = volumes); volatile; volcanic; voluntary; volunteer
VOP	Very Old Port; very oldest procurable (port, brandy etc)
VP	Vice President; vanishing point; variable pitch; verb phrase; vent pipe; Vice-Principal
vp	vanishing point; variable pitch
VPC	*vente par correspondence* = French mail order
vpd	vehicles per day (**vph** = vehicles per hour; **vpm** = vehicles per mile)
VPL	visible panty line
VPO	Vienna Philharmonic Orchestra
Vpo	Valparaiso
V Pres	Vice-President
vps	vibrations per second
VR	*Victoria Regina* = Queen Victoria; Volunteer Reserve; velocity ratio; virtual reality; voltage regulator; vulcanised rubber
VRAM	video random access memory (computers)
VRB, vrb	variable (meteorology)
VRC	Victoria Racing Club, Melbourne; Volunteer Rifle Corps
V Rev	Very Reverend
vrg	veering (meteorology)
VRI	*Victoria Regina et Imperatrix* = Victoria, Queen and Empress
VRO	vehicle registration office
VS, vs	veterinary surgeon; variable speed; *vide supra* = see above; volatile solid; *volti subito* = turn over quickly
vs	*versus* = against (eg England vs West Indies)
VSAM	virtual storage access method (computers)
VSB, vsb	vestigial sideband (telecommunications); qv **VSM**
VSCC	Vintage Sports Car Club

VSD	ventricular septal defect; vendor's shipping document
VSI	vertical speed indicator
V-sign	Index and middle fingers held up and spread to indicate victory
VSL	venture scout leader
VSM	vestigial sideband modulation (qv **VSB**)
VSO	very superior old (port, brandy etc); Vienna State Opera; Voluntary Service Overseas
VSOP	very superior old pale (port, brandy etc)
VSR	very special reserve (wine); very short range
VST	Virtual Studio Technology (computer composing)
VSTOL	vertical and short takeoff and landing (aircraft)
VT, vt	variable time; variable transmission; ventricular tachycardia
VTC	Volunteer Training Corps
vtg	voting
VTL	variable threshold logic (computers)
VTO	vertical takeoff (aircraft)
VTOHL	vertical takeoff, horizontal landing (aircraft)
VTOL	vertical takeoff and landing (aircraft)
VTOVL	vertical takeoff, vertical landing (aircraft)
VTR	videotape recorder/recording
VU	volume unit (acoustics)
Vul	Vulgate (also **Vulg**)
vv	vice versa; viva voce
VVL	visible vest line (see VPL)
VVO	very, very old (port, brandy etc)
VW	Very Worshipful; Volkswagen = literally, German people's car (German car make)
VWF	vibration white finger (debilitating miner's disease caused by prolonged exposure to drill vibration)
VX	Lethal nerve gas (US)

W

W ... DOUBLE U

W	Wales; Welsh; watt (also **w**); Wednesday; West; Western; white; widow; widowed; wide; women's size (clothing); warden; Wesleyan
w	waist; war; warm; water; watt; weather; west; wet; week; weight; white; wicket (cricket); wide (cricket); width; wife; wind; wire; with; widow; widower; win; won; woman; work
WA	West Africa; Western Australia; Westminster Abbey
WAAA	Women's Amateur Athletic Association
WAAAF	Women's Auxiliary Australian Air Force

WAAC	Women's Army Auxiliary Corps
WAAF	Women's Auxiliary Air Force
WAAS	Women's Auxiliary Army Force
WAC	Women's Army Corps (US)
WACB	World Association for Christian Broadcasting
WACCC	Worldwide Air Cargo Commodity Classification
Wad	Wadham College, Oxford (also **Wadh**)
WADF	Western Air Defense (US)
WAE, wae	when actually employed
WAF, waf	with all faults
WAFFLE	wide angle fixed field locating equipment
W Afr	West Africa
WAGGGS	World Association of Girl Guides and Girl Scouts
WAIS	Wechsler Adult Intelligence Scale; **WAIS-R** = Wechsler Adult Intelligence Scale – Revised (qv **WISC, WISC-R**)
Wal	Walloon
wam	wife and mother
w&i	weighing and inspection
W&M	William and Mary (architectural style, early 18th century)
w&s	whisky and soda
w&t	wear and tear
WAR	Women Against Rape
War	Warwickshire (also **Warks**); Warsaw
war	warrant; **warr** = warranty
WARC	World Alliance of Reformed Churches
warn	warning
WASA	Welsh Amateur Swimming Association
Wash	Washington
WASP	White Anglo-Saxon Protestant (also **Wasp**)
WAST	Western Australia Standard Time
Wat	Waterford
WAT curve	weight-altitude-temperature curve (aeronautics)
WATA	World Association of Travel Agencies
WATS	wide area telephone service

W Aus	Western Australia
WAVES	Women Accepted for Volunteer Emergency Service (US Navy)
WAYC	Welsh Association of Youth Clubs
WB	Warner Brothers (Hollywood film studio); water Board; World Bank for Reconstruction and Development
wb, WB	water ballast; waste ballast; waveband; waybill; weekly benefits; westbound; wheelbase
WBA	World Boxing Association; West Bromwich Albion Football Club
WBC	World Boxing Council; white blood count/cell
WBF	World Bridge Federation
WBI	whole body irradiation
wbi	will be issued
WBS	whole body scan
WBT	wet-bulb temperature
WC	War Cabinet; water closet; West-Central postal district of London; working capital; workmens' compensation
wc	water closet; water cock; without charge; wheelchair
W/C	Wing Commander (also **W Cdr**)
WCA	Women's Christian Association; Wildlife and Countryside Act
WCAT	Welsh College of Advanced Technology
WCC	War Crimes Commission; World Council of Churches
WCEU	World Christian Endeavour Union
WCF	World Congress of Faiths
WCL	World Confederation of Labour
WCP	World Council for Peace
WCT	World Championship Tennis
WCTU	Women's Christian Temperence Union (N America)
WCWB	World Coucil for the Welfare of the Blind
WD	War Department; well developed (also **w/d**); Works Department
wd	warranted (also **w/d**); wood; word; would

W/D	withdrawal
WDA	Welsh Development Agency; write-down analysis (tax)
WDC	War Damage Commission; Woman Detective Constable; World Data Centre
wdf	wood door and frame
WDM	wavelength division multiplex (telecommunications system)
WDS	Woman Detective Sergeant
WDV, wdv	written down value (tax)
w/e	weekend; week ending
WEA	Workers' Educational Association
wea	weather; weapon
WEC	World Energy Conference; wind energy converter
Wed	Wednesday (also **Weds**)
wef	with effect from
WEFC	West European Fisheries Conference
WEFT	wings, engine, fuselage, tail (aeronautics)
weld	welding
Well	Wellington, New Zealand
we'll	we will; we shall
we're	we are
weren't	were not
WES	World Economic Survey; Women's Engineering Society
west	western
Westm	Westminster
WET	Western European Time
we've	we have
Wex	Wexford
WF	white female; wave function; Wells Fargo
wf	wrong font (printing)
WFA	Women's Football Association; White Fish Authority
WFC	World Food Council
WFD	World Federation of the Deaf ·
WFEO	World Federation of Engineering Organisations

WFMH	World Federation for Mental Health
WFP	World Food Programme (UN)
WFPA	World Federation for the Protection of Animals
WFTU	World Federation of Trade Unions
WG	Welsh Guards; W G Grace (English cricketer, 1848-1915)
WGA	Writers' Guild of America
WGC	Welwyn Garden City, Hertfordshire
Wg/Cdr	Wing Commander
W Glam	West Glamorgan
WGU	Welsh Golfing Union
WH	White House (US); water heater; withholding also **w/h**)
Wh	watt hour (also **Whr**)
wh	wharf (also **whf**); which; white
WHA	World Hockey Association; World Health Assembly (UN)
W'hampton	Wolverhampton
whb	wash hand-basin
whf	wharf (also **wh**)
whfg	wharfage
WHO	World Health Organisation; White House Office (US)
WHOI	Woods Hole Oceanographic Institute
who'll	who will; who shall
who's	who is
WH question	A question beginning with *who, which, what, where, when* or *how,* designed to elicit information rather than 'yes' or 'no' answers
WHRA	World Health Research Centre
whsle	wholesale
WHT	William Herschel Telescope at La Palma
WI	Women's Institute; West Indies; West Indian; Windward Islands
wi	wrought iron; when issued (finance)
WIA	wounded in action
Wick	· Wicklow
wid	widow; widower

WIF	West Indies Federation
Wig	Wigtown, Scotland
wigig	when it's gone, it's gone (retailing term)
WILCO	will comply (radio signal)
Wilts	Wiltshire
WIMP	windows, icons, menus, pointers (computer screen display system)
WIN	Windows, Microsoft's operating system
Winch	Winchester
W Ind	West Indies; West Indian
Wing Cdr	Wing Commander
WINGS, Wings	warrants in negotiable government securities
Winn	Winnipeg, Canada
wint	winter
WIP	work in progress; waste incineration plant
WIPO	World Intellectual Property Organisation
WIRDS	weather information reporting and display system
WISC	Wechsler Intelligence Scale for Children; **WISC-R** = Wechsler Intelligence Scale for Children – Revised
WISP	wide-range imaging spectrometer
wit	witness
WITA	Women's International Tennis Association
Wits	Witwatersrand, South Africa
WJC	World Jewish Congress
WJEC	Welsh Joint Education Committee
wk	week; weak; well known; work; wreck
wkg	working
wkly	weekly
wkr	worker
wks	weeks; works
wkt	wicket (cricket); **wkt kpr** = wicketkeeper
WL	waiting list; water line; West Lothian; *wagon-lit* = railway sleeping car; Women's Liberation; wavelength (also **w/l**)
WLA	Women's Land Army
wld	would

wldr	welder
WLHB	Women's League of Health and Beauty
WLM	Women's Liberation Movement
WLPSA	Wild Life Preservation Society of Australia
WLR	Weekly Law Reports
WLTM	Would Love To Meet (used in personal classified ads)
WLUS	World Land Use Survey
WM	white male; war memorial; watt-meter; wire mesh
WMA	World Medical Association
WMAA	Whitney Museum of American Art, New York
WMC	Ways and Means Committee; working men's club; World Meteorological Centre; World Methodist Council
wmk	watermark (papermaking, philately)
WMO	World Meteorological Organisation
wmp	with much pleasure
WMS	World Magnetic Survey
wndp	with no down payment
WNE	Welsh National Eisteddfod
WNL, wnl	within normal limits
WNO	Welsh National Opera
WNP	Welsh Nationalist Party
WO	War Office; Warrant Officer; welfare officer; wireless operator; walkover; written order
w/o	without; written off
WOAR	Women Organised Against Rape
wob	white on black (graphics); washed overboard
WOC	waiting on cement (**WOCS** = waiting on cement to set)
woc	without compensation
woe	without equipment
WOG	Wrath of God Syndrome (AIDS)
wog	water, oil or gas; with other goods
wogs	workers on government service
Wolfs	Wolfson College, Oxford
Wolves	Wolverhampton Wanderers Football Club

WOMAN	World Organisation for Mothers of All Nations
won't	will not
WOO	World Oceanographic Organisation
wop	with other property
WOR	without our responsibility
Wor	Worshipful (also **Wp**)
Worc	Worcester College, Oxford
Worcs	Worcestershire
WORM	write once, read many times (computers)
wouldn't	would not
WOW	Women Against Ordination of Women; waiting on weather
wowser	Reputedly, *We Only Want Social Evils Removed* – Australian term for someone devoted to the abolition of alcohol and the reform of alcoholics and drinkers
WP	Western Province (S Africa); West Point (US); White Paper; without prejudice; word processor; working party
wp	waste paper; waste pipe; weather permitting; wild pitch (baseball); will proceed; word processor
WPA	Water Polo Association; Works Projects Administration (US, 1935-43); World Pool-Billiards Association; World Presbyterian Alliance
wpb	waste paper basket
WPBSA	World Professional Billiards and Snooker Association
WPC	Woman Police Constable
wpe	white porcelain enamel
wpg	waterproofing
WPGA	Women's Professional Golfers' Association
WPI	World Press Institute; wholesale price index
wpm	words per minute (keyboard typing speed)
WPRL	Water Pollution Research Laboratory
wps	with prior service

WR	West Riding, Yorkshire; Western Region; *Willelmus Rex* = King William; Wassermann reaction (VD test)
wr	water repellent; war risk (insurance); warehouse receipt
WRA	Water Research Association; Wisley Rose Award (Royal Horticultural Society)
WRAAC	Women's Royal Australian Army Corps
WRAAF	Women's Royal Australian Air Force
WRAC	Women's Royal Army Corps
WRAF	Women's Royal Air Force
WRANS	Women's Royal Australian Naval Service
WRC	Water Research Council
WRE	Weapons Research Establishment (Australia)
w ref	with reference
WRI	war risks insurance
WRNR	Women's Royal Naval Reserve
WRNS	Women's Royal Naval Service (Wrens)
wro	war risks only (insurance)
WRP	Worker's Revolutionary Party
WRU	Welsh Rugby Union
WRVS	Women's Royal Voluntary Service
WS	water-soluble; wind speed; weapon system
W Sam	Western Samoa
WSC	World Series Cricket
WSCF	World Student Christian Federation
WSJ	*Wall Street Journal* (US)
WSM	Women's Suffrage Movement
wsp	water supply point
WSSA	Welsh Secondary Schools Association
W star	Wolf-Rayet star (also **WR star**)
WSTN	World Service Television News
WT	withholding tax; wireless telegraphy (also **W/T**)
wt	weight; warrant; watertight
WTA	Women's Tennis Association; World Transport Agency; winner takes all
WTAA	World Trade Alliance Association

wtd	warranted
WTG	wind turbine generator
wthr	weather
WTN	Worldwide Television News
WTO	Warsaw Treaty Organisation; World Tourism Organisation
wtr	winter; writer
WTT	World Team Tennis
WTTA	Wholesale Tobacco Trade Association (of GB and N Ireland)
WTUC	World Trade Union Conference
WU	Western Union
WUJS	World Union of Jewish Students
WUPJ	World Union for Progressive Judaism
WUS	World University Service
w/v	weight to volume ratio; water valve (also **wv**)
WVA	World Veterinary Association
WVF	World Veterans' Federation
WW	worldwide
w/w	weight for weight; wall-to-wall (carpets); white wall (tyres)
WW1	World War One (1914-18)
WW2	World War Two (1939-45) Also **WWII**
WWF	World Wildlife Fund (now Worldwide Fund for Nature)
WWMCCS	World Wide Military Command and Control System
WWO	Wing Warrant Officer
WWSSN	worldwide standard seismograph network
WWSU	World Water Ski Union
WWW	World Weather Watch; *Who Was Who* (yearbook); world wide web
WX	women's extra large (clothing size)
WYR	West Yorkshire Regiment
wysiwyg	what you see is what you get (computer to printer)
Wz	*Warenzeichen* = German trademark
WZO	World Zionist Organisation

X	Roman numeral for 10; 'Adults Only' motion picture certificate (now '18' symbol); symbol for a location on maps; ballot paper choice; a kiss; a cross (eg King's X = King's Cross); an error; a variable; an unknown factor; an illiterate signature; an extension (eg X123 for a phoneline)
x	symbol for multiplication (maths); variable (algebra); extra; coordinate; hoar-frost (meteorology)
xan	xanthene; xanthic (chemistry)
XAS	X-ray absorption spectroscopy
xb	ex-bonus
xc	ex capitalisation; ex coupon (also **xcp**)
X-chromosome	Sex chromosome in female humans and many animals (qv **Y-chromosome**)
xcl	excess current liabilities
XCT	X-ray computed tomography
xd	ex-dividend (also **xdiv**)
x'd	deleted, crossed-out (also **x'd out**)
Xer	Xerox copier or reproduction
XES	X-ray emission spectroscopy
XFA	X-ray fluorescence analysis (also **XRFA**)
XI	X-ray imaging

xi	ex-interest (also **x in**)
XJ	Range of Jaguar cars (introduced 1968)
XL	extra large (clothing size)
X, les	ex-students of the *Ecole Polytechnique*
xlwb	extra-long wheel base
XM	experimental missile
XMS	extended memory specification (computers)
Xn	Christian (**Xnty** = Christianity)
XO	executive officer; fine cognac (brandy)
XP	First two Greek letters (*khi, rho*) of *Khristos* = Christ; express paid
xpl	explosive; explosion
X-position	Position in sexual intercourse (described in Dr Alex Comfort's *The Joy of Sex* but ultimately impossible to illustrate adequately)
XPS	X-ray photoelectron spectroscopy
Xr	examiner
X-rated	Unofficial classification for adult movies and videos
X-ray	Short wavelength electromagnetic radiation (also **x-ray**)
XRD	X-ray diffraction
x rd	crossroad (**x rds** = crossroads)
XRE	X-ray emission
XRM	X-ray mammography
XRMA	X-ray microphobe analysis
XRT	X-ray topography
xs, ex's	expenses
Xt	Christ
x-unit	unit of length of wavelengths of gamma – and x-rays
XX	double strength ale (**XXX** = triple strength; **XXXX** = quadruple strength, or 3.9% alcohol by weight)
XXXX	euphemism for four-letter words
xyl	xylophone
XYZ	examine your zipper

Y

Y	Japanese yen; Chinese yuan; Yugoslavia; short for **YMCA, YWCA**, etc – qv
y	yard; yacht; year; yellow; young; youngest; variable (algebra); dry air (meteorology); symbol for any unknown factor (as in *xy*)
YA	young adult
YAG	yttrium-aluminium garnet (artificial diamond)
YAL	Young Australia League
Y&LR	York and Lancaster Regiment
Y&R	Young and Rubicam (advertising agency)
YAR	York-Antwerp Rules (marine insurance)
Yard, The	Scotland Yard
YAS	Yorkshire Agricultural Society
YAVIS	young, attractive, verbal, intelligent, successful (ideal profile)
YB, yb	yearbook
YC	Young Conservative; yacht club; Yale College (US); youth club
YCA	Youth Camping Association
Y-chromosome	Sex chromosome in male humans and many male animals
Y2K	Second millennium; year 2000
YCL	Young Communist League
YCW	Young Christian Workers; you can't win

yd	yard (**yds** = yards)
YE	Your Excellency
yel	yellow
Yem	Yemen; Yemeni
YEO	Youth Employment Officer
yer	yearly effective rate of interest
YES	Youth Employment Service; Youth Enterprise Scheme
YFC	Young Farmers' Club
YFG	yttrium-ferrite garnet (qv **YAG**, **YIG**)
Y-fronts	style of men's underpants, having a Y opening
YH	youth hostel
YHA	Youth Hostels Association
YHANI	Youth Hostels Association of Northern Ireland
YHWH	consonant letters of the Hebrew name for God (*Yahweh* or Jehovah), regarded as too sacred to be pronounced (also **YHVH**, **JHVH**, **JHWH**)
Yid	Yiddish; Yiddisher; derogatory name for a Jew
YIG	yttrium-iron garnet (qv **YFG**, **YAG**)
Yippie	Youth International Party member
YMBA	Yacht and Motor Boat Association
YMCA	Young Men's Christian Association
YMCU	Young Men's Christian Union
YMFS	Young Men's Friendly Society
YMHA	Young Men's Hebrew Association
YMV	yellow mosaic virus
yo	year-old (eg a 2-yo stallion)
YOB, yob	year of birth
YOC	Young Ornithologists' Club (RSPB)
YOD, yod	year of death
YOM, yom	year of marriage
YOP	Youth Opportunities Programme
Yorks	Yorkshire
you're	you are
you've	you have
YP	young person; young prisoner
YPA	Young Pioneers of America

yr	year; your; younger
YRA	Yacht Racing Association
yrbk	yearbook
yrly	yearly
yrs	years; yours (also **Yrs**)
YS	Young Socialists
Ys	Yugoslavia; Yugoslavian (also **Yugo**)
YT	Yukon Territory
YTD, ytd	year to date
YTS	Youth Training Scheme
YTYTK	'You're too young to know!' (catchphrase from ITMA radio show)
Yugo	Yugoslavia; Yugoslavian car brand
Yuk	Yukon
yuppie	young upwardly mobile professional (profile)
YWCA	Young Women's Christian Association
YWCTU	Young Women's Christian Temperence Union
YWHA	Young Women's Hebrew Association
YWS	Young Wales Society

Zip

America's Zip Code (**Zip** = Zone Improvement Plan) was conceived in 1963 as a postcode of 37,000 five-digit numbers, each representing a geographical area in the US, to facilitate mail sorting and delivery. It has now grown to a nine-digit, two-section code number (eg 11577-6127) which all residents are urged to attach to their addresses. Not too surprisingly, very few residents comply. Britain's postcode achieves the same geographical definition with a fairly easily remembered combination of six letters and numbers.

Z	Zairian zaire (currency); zero; Zionist; *Zoll* = German Customs
z	zero; zenith; zone; symbol for haze (meteorology); variable (algebra)
Zag	Zagreb, Croatia
Zam	Zambia
Zan	Zanzibar
ZANU	Zimbabwe African National Union
ZAPU	Zimbabwe African People's Union
ZB	Zen Buddhist
zD	*zum Beispiel* = for example, eg
Z car	police patrol car ('zulu' = radio call sign for Z); **Z cars**: a long-running TV series first broadcast in 1962

Z chart	business chart accumulating daily, weekly and monthly totals
ZD	zenith distance (astronomy)
ZEBRA	zero-energy breeder reactor assembly
Zeep	zero-energy experimental pile
ZEG	zero economic growth
zen	zenith
ZENITH	zero-energy nitrogen-heated thermal reactor
zero-g	zero gravity
ZETA	zero-energy thermonuclear assembly
ZETR	zero-energy thermonuclear reactor
ZF, zf	zero frequency
ZG	zoological gardens
ZH	zero hour
zH	*zu Handen* = care of, c/o
ZIF	zero insertion force (electronics)
ZIFT	zygote intrafallopian transfer (infertility treatment)
ZIP, zip	zone improvement plan; **zip code** = US postcode
Zl	Polish zloty
zod	zodiac
zoo	zoological gardens
zool	zoology; zoological; zoologist
ZPG	zero population growth
ZSI	Zoological Society of Ireland
ZST	Zone Standard Time (**ZT** = zone time)
Ztg	*Zeitung* = German newspaper (**Zs** = *Zeitschrift* = magazine)
Zur	Zurich, Switzerland
ZZ	UK vehicle registration letters for temporarily imported cars
zzzz	sleep; snoozing

And, finally . . . AAA (Abolition of Acronymic Abominations)

To many people nothing is more annoying than those cute, self-consciously created and usually ephemeral acronyms, of which there are perhaps more than one would have wished in this book.

This widespread irritation has, on occasions, erupted in (mostly tongue-in-cheek) protests against acronyms, typically expressed acronymically. Here are a few would-be anti-acronym campaigns and organisations:

COCOA	Council to Outlaw Contrived and Outrageous Acronyms (from a 1977 *Punch* cartoon)
DRAG	Diminish Reliance on Acronyms Generally (*New York Times*)
SEA	Society for the Elimination of Acronyms

and a couple more, reported (or invented) by Don Hauptman in his *Acronymania*:

AAAAAA	Association for the Alleviation of Asinine Abbreviations and Absurd Acronyms
CRAP	Committee to Resist Acronymic Proliferation

Collins Wordpower

English is the most widely used language in the world, yet it is also one of the easiest languages to be misunderstood in. The Collins Wordpower series is the ultimate in user-friendliness for all who have wished for an authoritative, comprehensive yet accessible range of guides through the maze of English usage. Designed for ease of use and illustrated by top cartoonists, these books will enrich your powers of communication – whether in speech, writing, comprehension or general knowledge – and they are fun to use!

PUNCTUATION
0 00 472373 2
How to handle the "nuts and bolts" of English prose £5.99

GOOD GRAMMAR
0 00 472374 0
How to break down the barriers between you and clear communication £5.99

SUPER SPELLER
0 00 472371 6
How to master the most difficult-to-spell words and names in the English language £5.99

GOOD WRITING
0 00 472381 3
How to write clear and grammatically correct English £5.99

VOCABULARY EXPANDER
0 00 472382 1
How to dramatically increase your word power £5.99

ABBREVIATIONS
0 00 472389 9
The complete guide to abbreviations and acronyms £5.99

FOREIGN PHRASES
0 00 472388 0
The most commonly used foreign words in the English language £5.99

WORD CHECK
0 00 472378 3
How to deal with difficult and confusable words £5.99